Where Do You Draw the Line?
By
Louis Harding
ISBN: 978-1-9162285-2-8

Now a Major TV Series on Channel Five

i2i Publishing, Manchester.
www.i2ipublishing.co.uk

Chapter One

The car was small, cramped and hot. Outside, it was thirty degrees, and that was at night. But that wasn't the reason I was sweating.

I was co-presenting my first major documentary on national television and hoping to conduct an interview on camera with the man who was next to me in the back of the car. He seemed to be relaxed. But then, why wouldn't he be? He was the one carrying a loaded gun.

It was in that moment, looking at the gun that a Colombian man I'd never met before had stuffed into his waistband, that I started wondering how the hell I had ended up 5,000 miles from Manchester in one of Colombia's most dangerous cities and, more importantly, if I might ever get home.

A few weeks earlier, I'd been back in the land of *Coronation Street* and cups of tea, minding my own business. I'd applied for several reality TV shows in the past, but in this case, I'd just received an Instagram message from a casting producer. Usually I'd get contact from dating shows, but this time it was something completely different.

'We're looking for contributors to take part in a brand-new TV documentary. We will be following recreational cocaine users along a journey to South America for an experience of a lifetime.'

At this point most people would probably think 'Cocaine?' that's nothing to do with me.'

But my thought was, 'Shit!' Why do they think I'm a recreational user? Why on earth would they want to take me to South America?' It sounded like some sort of Jeremy Kyle abroad, but I asked for more details. I mean, who wouldn't? I've always been inquisitive by nature.

I received an application form the following day. Some of the questions on there were a bit personal, and slightly off-putting. Should I press 'send' and apply? Fuck it. I did.

Two days later, I received an email asking if I was free to have a chat with one of the casting producers, kind of like a telephone interview, I suppose. Knowing I'm confident on the phone, I thought I'd smash it.

A few hours later, my phone rang. It was one of the producers. The call started out quite chilled. They casually asked me to tell them a bit about myself - it was very easy-going. Then the questions ramped up a bit.

'What are your thoughts on cocaine?'

At first, I was a little thrown. I had to be honest. 'I just see cocaine as a party drug and nothing more.'

Then it got a bit deeper.

'Have you ever used cocaine in the past?'

I responded, 'Yeah, I've taken it at festivals and house parties 'n' stuff.'

I didn't know fully what I was getting myself into, but I came off the call thinking that the project could be a life-changing experience. My only concern was that this went beyond reality TV. It was actual reality and it involved my family.

Cocaine wasn't something I'd ever talked about around my loved ones, so to potentially go on TV and talk about it worried me. They're completely against any drugs, so for me to tell them that there was now a chance I was going to South America to film a documentary about cocaine would completely throw them. It wasn't only the drugs part of it but travelling to a Continent known for crime and violence, that's a lot for any parent to think about.

I think they'd always had an idea that I'd tried coke in the past. It had just never been brought up in conversation. I was going to have to find the right time to tell them about it.

A few days later, I received another email. It was the producers inviting me to a Skype audition.

'This is the next stage of the process for our new documentary which will be filmed in Colombia.'

Shit! In Colombia? I ran downstairs and rang my mate, over the moon at what I might be doing. Who gets the opportunity to travel to Colombia with a TV crew and film a documentary on cocaine? Not literally 'on cocaine', but you get my drift.

On one hand, something was telling me this could be the start of something big and on the other, I was worried that I would be portrayed as some sort of cocaine addict or heavy user, which I knew I wasn't.

I rang my mam to tell her the news.

'Mum, you'll never guess what! I've got a Skype interview with a TV production company.' Then I panicked. What could I say? 'They're filming about life in Colombia and its differences to the UK.'

She said, 'Brilliant, sounds great! Wait… did you just say Colombia? It's very dangerous over there, you know.'

I remember putting the phone down thinking, 'Why have I just lied about the whole thing?'

Before I did the Skype interview, I knew that I'd need to make it clear to the production company that I probably wasn't the right person for the show if they were looking for the typical so-called 'druggy'. I knew that I could add something, being a down-to-earth lad who likes to have a bit of fun every now and then, but I also had my livelihood to protect.

I'm confident, but before that Skype call, I was as nervous as hell. Despite those nerves, I took the call and found myself chatting to a complete stranger about my past experiences on cocaine. It felt odd. The questions started out quite chilled, 'What do you think of the drug?' and 'How many times have you used it?'. They got tougher to answer after each question. I'd answered honestly, yet in my head, I was thinking, 'I wonder what my Mum and Dad would think of all this?'

I knew that if I got on the show, there was no hiding it.

The Skype call went well, and the producer said I had a great energy and a bubbly personality. I was told that they would edit the interview down to a couple of minutes and show it to the directors. Everything moved so quickly. Four days before, I was getting a message through on Instagram. Suddenly, I was chatting to a producer on Skype about my past drug experiences.

A week later, I was on the show. I was buzzing. I was excited - all the feelings to which regular cocaine users might have felt after sniffing a line. But this was a natural high; the feeling of anticipation at what might happen when I came face to face with dangerous individuals in the name of television entertainment.

I knew from my experience filming TV shows that a lot of the details would be left until the last minute, but the conversation I needed to have with my Mam and Dad was getting closer. That was when the producers 'solved' all my problems with one idea - they planned to interview my parents on screen.

Chapter Two

Surely, my parents would understand the reasons I was interested in doing the documentary. I just didn't know how to put it to them. I'm a man, and I'm 26. I did the only thing I knew. I put it off until the moment was right on top of me and we were sat around the table at teatime.

When I told them that I'd be taking part in the show pending certain 'checks', they were over the moon. They saw it as a huge opportunity, just like I did. They knew that I'd been on reality shows in the past and that they hadn't really worked out. This would be different.

Just as I was about to leave the dinner table, I gave them a little hint.

'It's going to be mad filming a documentary about cocaine, isn't it?'

My mum's eyes rolled. 'What do you mean a documentary about cocaine?'

I finally told her all I knew about the show, leaving out the part where I'd taken cocaine on nights out. No real man can lie to his mother's face and I'm no different. I could see she was fuming. She didn't fully understand the reasons I was picked, but then neither did I at that stage.

I then received a call on my phone from a private number, and at that point, I knew it was going to be either someone trying to sell me PPI or the casting producer.

'Hi Louis, I'm pleased to say that the channel commissioners thought you were great. They would love to have you on the show.'

Part of me was buzzing, but the other half of my heart sank. I still wasn't 100% sure about doing the show, but this was the moment. I am not the type to back out of things, and I wasn't going to now.

It took just four days for everything to be confirmed with the production team.

I was told the main objective of the documentary was to explore the world of cocaine. The series would be three one-hour episodes which would be aired on Channel 5. National television. I agreed to take part. They spoke about filming dates, activities we might do whilst in Colombia and what they'd like from the show. There would be just over a week filming in the UK before leaving, two weeks in Colombia and a further week of filming once we'd returned.

I remember thinking 'If we arrive back.' Yet I agreed to take part.

A few days later and the emails started flooding in - contracts, dates and times. Everything started moving so quickly. One email stood out: 'Please be aware that prior to travelling to Colombia you will be required to take several vaccinations.'

I told my family that I was 100% committed. I was going to Colombia. Knowing that I might never get an experience like it again, they agreed. Their worry was how I was going to be portrayed due to the nature of the show. I understood exactly how they felt.

A few days later the series senior editor, Marc, called me. I think they'd gathered from my attitude on the phone that I had a few worries about doing the show. He agreed to come to Manchester for a chat to discuss the show at length. I'd openly admitted that I'd taken cocaine in the past, but I was worried they had the wrong end of a sharp stick.

When he arrived a few days later he explained a bit more about the show and the things I could be potentially doing whilst in Colombia. Things were mentioned like going into the jungle to see how cocaine is made, and even interviewing cartel members. But there was something even scarier to me at the time - they wanted to interview my Mum and Dad on camera!

Marc then told me that I'd be joined on the trip by three other contributors. That worried me slightly and I wasn't sure why, but I knew that I'd soon find out. As the conversation continued, I was still a little confused as to what type of person they wanted for the show, so I asked him.

The response was a good one. 'We're looking for normal people who have openly admitted taking cocaine in the past and are not afraid to talk about it.'

After the conversation, I felt ten times better. I signed the contract and after two weeks of sleepless nights thinking about the journey ahead, I received my train ticket to London. The plan was to film my initial interview there, meet the other contributors, film some of the opening scenes and then head back to Manchester to prep for Colombia. London was going to be my home for a good few days.

The only time I'd ever been to London was for meetings. The first time I went I was 19 or 20, and that was for a previous TV show. I've never been to the capital as a tourist. It had always been rush here; rush there and then set off straight back home.

As I set off on the train journey from rainy Manchester, I started to think what the other three presenters were going to be like. With the show focusing on cocaine, and the related underworld, I thought I might have been the black sheep of the group. I didn't want to turn up in London on the first day to meet three absolute nutters.

I called my Mum on the train and explained my concerns. Her reply was as blunt as it was true.

'They're probably thinking the same thing about you!'

Two hours later, I arrived at Euston station. As I made my way to the studio, I didn't take in any of it - the red buses, the tourist attractions, the London landmarks that colour most tourist impressions of the UK. All I could think about was Colombia. London was a crazy place, but I had a strong feeling the capital of cocaine was going to be a lot crazier.

My instincts were spot on.

Chapter Three

After a short tube trip, I arrived at the studio and noticed a few people stood outside the entrance smoking. I had no time to prepare myself. The only familiar face I could see was Marc, the senior editor of the series, who had visited me in Manchester. The closer I got, the faster my heart was beating. The nerves were obviously kicking in.

It was my first time meeting the production team, so I knew I had to be super confident. I walked over and shouted in my Mancunian accent, 'Hello, Nice to meet you all!' Surprisingly, every single one of them was really welcoming. Not that I knew who they were.

Marc then showed me upstairs into the dressing room. He quickly ran through the plan for the day, informing me that my master interview would be in thirty minutes. After the long train journey, I was kind of happy that I had a bit of time to chill.

I was sat there in a luxury dressing room scrolling through Twitter, feet-up, thinking that I could get used to this lifestyle. However, the longer I sat waiting, the more nervous I became.

Suddenly, I heard a strong Bristolian accent. I looked up.

'Hello, my dear, I'm Chanel, you all right, my lover?' I remember thinking 'Jeeez!' This girl looks like some sort of Colombian gangster. She had tattoos everywhere, mixed race with a skin fade. A real distinct look about her.

'Hi, I'm Louis, Nice to meet ya! You good?'

I couldn't work out if she was one of the contributors or she was part of the crew, but there was no time to chat. Common sense said she was one of the other contributors, but I still wasn't 100%. Before I had a chance to find out, Marc walked back into the dressing room and told me that they were ready for me in the studio. Time for my close-up.

I'd never done a documentary before; it had always been dating or reality shows. Actual reality? Drug deals, cartels, hitmen, fixers, gangster-looking co-presenters? I was in at the deep-end, and when the camera is on you, you either sink or swim.

The first thing I asked the crew when I got into the studio was who was Chanel. It turned out she *was* one of the three other presenters that I'd be with on the show. I'd be sharing the screen with a very large character and she'd definitely made a statement. I knew I had my work cut out if my personality was to come across.

The TV industry is 100% competitive. At times, you catch yourself hoping the others are quiet so that you can get your personality across - it's that cut-throat. You've got to be as loud as possible and get yourself noticed or you're not going to get anywhere. In reality TV in general, everyone wants to be the next star. You've got to put yourself out there, but not so much that you seem fake.

Previously I've been on other shows, but they all had common denominators; they were often set in the sun and about meeting up with girls and dating or drinking. After the final reality show I did before we went to Colombia - a dating show – I gave up on it all.

When channels asked me to take part, I turned them down, saying I was busy on other things. I look back at that now and think 'Why did I put myself in that position?', but it all fell into place. When this documentary came along, it was an opportunity to progress. It wasn't the same as the reality TV I'd known. The team on this documentary was very different.

Marc introduced me to the two series directors, Johnny and George. They would both be joining me on the trip to Colombia, so they were vital. Although directors are often associated with acting, and directing actors, the director is just as important on a reality television programme as a staged production of Macbeth. Both Johnny and George would be in overall control of what we did and where we went to do it. As an actor might rely on their film director for a final word on exactly how they should act, so would we, and I liked them both immediately.

It was the first time I'd been on camera for a while, so I was a little nervous. I sat down in the chair they had prepared in the corner of the room.

There was no turning back now. This would be the first piece of footage the public would see of me, and if first impressions are as important as everyone always says, the next fifteen seconds of celluloid exposure was vital to make a connection with the viewing public.

No pressure, then.

Chapter Four

I had a rough idea of how it was going to work. The directors would fire off a load of questions and I would answer them in full sentences. You get used to it after a while, and although the first time it makes you sound like you've got difficulties replying like a human being, as if you need to remind yourself of the question, after a while it becomes natural. You just have to remember to snap out of it at home. When your mam asks you if you want a cuppa and you reply, 'I'd really like a cup of tea', then you start getting salt added to it instead of sugar.

Suddenly everywhere went pitch black, the bright camera lights turned on and all the focus was on me. The questions started, and they were very similar to the ones asked on Skype a few weeks earlier. The one which stood out was. 'What are your thoughts on the possibility of meeting with criminals who are involved in the cocaine trade?'

I swallowed heavily.

'I'm quite excited to be honest - the thought of meeting a Colombian gangster was always on my bucket list!'

I remember asking myself at the time why I was joking about what could, and probably would, become reality in Colombia.

With the nature of the show, you had to be yourself, and I wanted to be as genuine as possible and prove that I wasn't a bad person because I've taken cocaine in the past. Most of the time, it was just me, Louis from Manchester. None of the interviews would be planned or orchestrated and that was what was so intriguing.

After an hour of the directors grilling me, the interview finally finished. I'd got through it without any other major fuckups; but I left the studio unsure about the whole thing. I just had a doubt in the back of my mind.

As I was walking back into the dressing room one of the cameramen shouted through the door, 'Good Job, Louis'. That was my inspiration to say, 'You know what, fuck it, let's do it!'

A few minutes later, Marc walked in.

'Louis, we've booked a cab to pick you up shortly. Here are your hotel details. The other three contributors are staying there as well, so if you bump into Chanel who you met earlier, maybe she can introduce you to the rest of the team? We will be going out for some food around 8pm so let's meet at reception for 7.45?'

I looked at my watch and it was 4pm already! The day had flown by. There was probably just enough time to get some food and get my head down for an hour ready for the night ahead.

After fifty minutes stuck in London traffic I'd finally arrived at the hotel. Still no food, no sleep and feeling grotty. As I stepped out the taxi, I heard someone shouting; 'Louuuuuuu!'

It was Chanel. Usually I'm shocking at remembering people I've literally just met, but there was no way I was going to forget that strong Bristolian accent, skin fade and tattoos. She stumbled out of the taxi she'd just arrived in with another girl.

'How did your interview go? Oh, by the way, meet Amber, she's one of the other presenters.'

As much as I wanted to speak to both of them, it had been a long day. The last thing I wanted was to be stood outside talking in the rain. I wanted to check-in, get some food and sleep for an hour. I told them I'd see them in reception for dinner and left them outside smoking.

By the look on Amber's face, I got the impression, Chanel was the crazy one of the group. I didn't really have time to work out Amber. She had a good vibe, was blonde and spoke well. You make little pocket judgements when you meet people fleetingly, don't you? But I immediately pegged Amber as the posh one in the group.

With one presenter still to be confirmed, I had no idea who it would be, and whether I'd be the only lad with three girls, or if it would be two girls and two guys. With the free time I had in my room, I drifted off to sleep wondering who might complete our quartet.

After a short sleep, I headed downstairs to reception. As I walked out of the lift, I noticed Amber and Chanel at the bar seating area. I could hear them giggling loudly. It was at that point I knew the whole experience was going to be a real laugh.

As I waited at the bar for a drink, I looked over my shoulder and noticed Amber strolling towards me. The way she was walking, I could tell she wasn't there to fuck about. She was there to do a job. There was a totally different feeling to meeting Amber compared to when I first met Chanel. That wasn't a bad thing, as after all, we were investigating a serious subject.

A few minutes later, the crew arrived in reception. George, Johnny and Marc greeted us all warmly, and there was a real feeling of setting out on a quest. The crew and directorial team gathered everyone around and told us that we'd be heading out for pizza. I was starving!

It was time for food.

As soon as we'd arrived at the restaurant, I ordered the biggest pizza on the menu. The atmosphere around the table was buzzing. George, one of our directors, raised his glass to everyone.

'Cheers - to making a great show.'

I whispered to Marc, who was sitting next to me, 'Aren't there supposed to be four of us?'

As if by coincidence, a young lad walked into the restaurant and joined us at the table. George kept his glass in the air.

'Meet Troi everyone, he will be joining us on the trip to Colombia, he is the fourth and final contributor.'

He looked like the typical uni grad lad in his early twenties. I knew straight away he was someone I would get along with. Every single one of us was completely different, but in a really good way.

After having earlier doubts about the show, my opinion started to change rapidly. We'd only known each other less than an hour and I already felt like I'd known them for years. Everyone was sound.

Two hours later, the first day was over and it was time to head back to the hotel. With the crew heading to bed, Chanel thought it would be a good idea to plant a seed in everyone's head, 'Anyone fancy a drink in the hotel bar?'

Despite just being told we had to be up for 8am for filming, I was never going to be the responsible one; 'Fuck it I'll have one, then I'm going to my room.'

Troi couldn't refuse and Amber followed suit. A few minutes later we found ourselves sat in the bar necking shots! That was the last thing I remembered of a very long day.

Chapter Five

When I woke up, pain swam to the surface quickest, followed by panic. What the hell had I been drinking last night? My head was banging, and it was the first full day of filming. After having such a good night, I'd woken up completely clueless. I turned over in bed and grabbed my phone lazily. There was a message from the crew.

'Please meet down at reception for 8am where we will have some breakfast and discuss the day ahead.'

Twenty minutes later, I'd showered and got ready. When I arrived at breakfast, I could tell the four of us was a little tender from the alcohol. As I tucked into a full English, the crew informed us of the plan for the day.

'Today you will be visiting South London University. We will be meeting a professor who specialises in drug testing. This can be anything from testing strength to finding out if any substances are being cut with the drugs.'

Before we'd arrived in London, we each provided a small sample of cocaine from a local dealer to the production team. Mad I know, but I was guessing it was time to find out the results. The samples had been sealed in bags and sent off to the laboratory for testing a few weeks earlier.

We were each from different sides of the country, so they wanted to compare the North to the South, the East to the West. There was nothing to say that I wouldn't have been charged when I went to get this gram of cocaine, if I was strong-armed by the law, but fortunately, that never happened. Although the laboratory tests were government approved and the sample would be destroyed after testing, it set a trend for most of the show; everything felt like it was on impulse. The programme makers wanted a surprise element. They kept everything so secretive.

I was a little nervous. Not only was it the first-time filming as a group but finding out the test results together felt slightly embarrassing. Having a slight hangover actually seemed to help the situation.

Upon arrival, we headed straight to the cafe for coffee all around. I looked to Troi.

'If I knew it was going to start so intensely, I wouldn't have drunk the night before.'

After several coffees, we made our way upstairs to the lab. It was the first time we would be speaking with someone who had a real knowledge of cocaine and what's inside the drug. It's something I'd wanted to know for a long time.

Again, I was concerned about how I was going to be portrayed. Buying a gram on a night out with the lads felt totally different to sending it off to a lab for testing and then being asked to discuss it on TV.

One of my mates said before I left Manchester; 'Find out what the fuck they put in it!' and now I had the chance. I'd heard stories in the past of people finding all sorts in their cocaine, from paracetamol to creatine and even cement or glass. I was trying not to imagine how embarrassing it would be if any of those materials were found in the sample I'd obtained.

As we walked into the lab we were asked to put on white overcoats, similar to the ones you wear at school in a science lesson. I looked like a professional scientist and the scene was set.

The professor walked in and introduced herself. Dr Kat was her name.

'Hi guys, this morning I will be talking you through the results of your individual cocaine samples sent into the lab. We're looking for anything which stands out and could be dangerous for human consumption. Is there anything you would like to ask me before I go ahead and start?'

There was a sudden silence around the room. Not a word from any of us. I think everyone was too eager to find out.

She continued, 'Ok, the first sample we are going to look at is a sample from Manchester.'

A dozen heads swivelled in my direction. In those moments, you're hyper-aware of being on screen. Knowing it was my sample I broke the ice.

'Go on, what is it you've found?'

Chanel couldn't stop giggling at me. She could probably see the panic in my face!

'So, the two things we found in the Manchester sample are caffeine and powdered sugar.'

I was a little surprised. I expected a lot worse and felt like I'd got off lightly. Maybe all the rumours of finding glass and other dodgy stuff was a myth? I still felt slightly embarrassed by it all, so much that even the camera crew noticed. I wasn't hiding anything, but I just felt slightly uncomfortable. I had to get over that barrier of talking about cocaine.

Troi was up next. He was the most chilled of us all. He looked more excited than nervous. Being the youngest of the group I kind of expected it. His sample contained exactly the same as mine. Powdered sugar and caffeine. It made sense. They were both white and looked identical to cocaine. I got the feeling that it was going to be found in all our samples.

I asked Dr Kat a question; 'Two of the four samples you've shown us so far contain sugar and caffeine. Is that usually what you find?'

The response I got turned in to a practical test. Two bowls were put in the centre of the table. One full of powdered sugar and one with caffeine. I was asked to dip my finger in both bowls and test it on my tongue. At first, I thought it was some sort of joke until I tried it. The taste was exactly the same as cocaine. I couldn't believe it.

Chanel was next. The results from Bristol were the same again. It was becoming obvious that the two products we had found were regularly used in the UK to cut cocaine.

Amber was last up. Dr Kat looked to Amber: 'Ok Amber. So, your sample is from London? We have found something very interesting in this sample.'

The room went silent. The four of us looked to Dr Kat in suspense.

'So, in this sample we've found Levamisole. It's quite an unusual find but it is becoming more common'. Chanel shouted, 'What the fuck is Levamisole?'

Dr Kat giggled, 'It's an animal deworming drug which is not suitable for human consumption.'

Amber couldn't believe it. 'What?!'

I could see in her face that she was really taken back by it, not only her but the four of us and the crew. Sugar and caffeine sounded bad enough but to then hear that one of the samples had something that wasn't even suitable for human consumption hit home. Everyone was aware that cocaine is cut with other products, but I guess none of us really thought too much into it.

We had all been sold different amounts but all less than a gram. My own sample had weighed in at 0.58g, very nearly half-measures. But at least my sample was 78.5% pure. Amber's sample, by comparison, weighed in at an almost accurate 0.97g. It was, however, only 46.6% pure and we all now knew what was in it.

It was the first time in the two days together that everyone was speechless. Dr Kat asked us individually what we thought of the findings. I felt quite dirty about it all so my response was short and simple. 'It's disgusting.'

It really gave me the incentive when in Colombia to find out why it's being mixed with these types of products and how? I had a feeling that the Colombians had some sort of input in it.

I had no idea how much.

Chapter Six

The day had turned out to be a lot more interesting than expected. As we headed back to the hotel for an early night there was so much to think about. Would people still want to take this drug knowing what's *really* in it?

The next day, we were back at the university to continue our studies with another professor. We were investigating the effects that cocaine (this time, the pure stuff) can have on your body. I knew some of the damage it could have on you physically, but I wasn't overly clued up on the mental side.

After arriving back at the university, it was straight into filming. The assembly hall was the location for the day. The four of us were told to take a seat at the front of the hall to await further instructions. I felt like I'd gone back ten years to school.

When I was younger, I'd been a proper little shit at school. I hadn't listened and found it a struggle in many ways. To be in a school hall as an adult, attentively taking in every word... well, it was a different experience.

The cameraman shouted 'Action!' and in walked the new professor, who introduced himself, and then presented his friend 'Charlie', who would help him with the demonstrations.

I was confused. He was the only person on the stage and none of the crew was called Charlie?

He continued: 'Charlie is the anatomy skull over on that table.'

The four of us burst out laughing. The name got everyone. I'm not sure if he called it Charlie on purpose but we couldn't stop giggling, so much that filming was delayed for ten minutes!

After several demonstrations showing how cocaine effects the brain, the Professor turned on the projector screen.

'Ok guys. I am now going to show you the heart monitor results from Chanel's night out.'

I heard Chanel whisper in my right ear, 'Well this could be interesting.'

I didn't have a clue what the professor was on about, never mind Chanel. 'What do they mean, heart monitor results?'

George overheard me asking Chanel. 'Don't worry about it now Louis, you'll find out soon.'

As part of an experiment, Chanel had been asked to wear a heart rate monitor on a night out, whilst on cocaine! I couldn't believe what I'd just been told. The crew could tell I was clearly unimpressed. I couldn't believe she'd agreed to do it, however, the results were in.

I looked up to the projector screen to see what I can only describe as a line-graph looking like the French alps. It was all over the place. It spiked up and down and I couldn't believe that it represented Chanel's heartbeat.

At one point in the night, her heartbeat had jumped from around eighty to one hundred and fifty-six in under two minutes. No one in the room could quite believe it. The professor told us it would take someone in the gym around thirty minutes working hard to get up to that heart rate.

Chanel was gobsmacked. She turned a shade of green. It was the first time that I'd seen her react to something without laughing. I think reality had finally kicked in. Seeing the results being that high obviously made her think long and hard about her future. Although she was brave, there was no way I was letting anyone monitor my heart rate on a night out.

That was a wrap for the day and again, it was another tough one. Filming daily was harder than I'd imagined. Not just physically, but mentally. I'd learnt so much over the three days that I was starting to forget what had happened.

It was then that I started to write daily notes on my experience, to remind myself of each step of the journey.

As we headed back to the hotel it was interesting hearing some of the conversations in the minibus. Amber was still pissed off to find that she had animal de-wormer in her cocaine sample. Chanel was still in shock over her heartrate results, while Troi and I remained a little confused. Finding out the sample results seemed to be playing on everyone's minds.

It had been a long three days in London. Some of the things I'd learnt weren't necessarily things I wanted to hear, but they were certainly interesting. There was a lot to take in and we were only just starting.

It was time to say goodbye to the crew and presenters. I'd have liked to say I was looking forward to going back to Manchester, yet I was enjoying it so much that I kind of wanted to stay. Knowing Colombia was less than a week away made it slightly easier to leave. There was so much to look forward to and the adventure was only just beginning.

Once I'd arrived back in Manchester, I still felt unsure what my role would be once we were in Colombia. With most of the filming in London focusing on the science side of cocaine surely, we were getting close to the interesting stuff. The criminal side.

A day later, I received a call from George. He asked if I was free to film for a day before leaving for Colombia. They wanted to create a bit of a back story for the documentary. Kind of like an opening scene explaining who I was, what I liked to do in my spare time, so that the viewers could get to know me.

'Yeah, I'm free, when is it you're thinking?'

George replied. 'Is tomorrow OK?'

I didn't even have time to think.

'Er, yeah that's fine. What sort of stuff is it you want to film?

He laughed; 'That's totally up to you mate - what do you get up to in your spare time?'

If you've never been to Old Trafford, then when you head to Manchester, you should go. With 76,000 fans on matchdays, it is the home of Manchester United Football Club, the most successful club in British football. I suggested we head there, as well as to five a-side football in the evening with my mates. The obvious follow on was a night out with the lads.

'That's great,' said George, 'Would your parents be happy filming with you?'

I panicked.

'What do you mean!?'

At first, I thought they was expecting my parents to join me and my mates on a night out. There was no chance I was having that. Apparently though, they just wanted to ask them a few questions about my life in general. Reluctantly I agreed.

I had just under twelve hours to get some of my mates together, organise a night out and then finally try and convince my mum and dad to film with me. All sorts of thoughts were going through my head. Are they going to embarrass me? Will my mates behave? Knowing that Chanel took cocaine on her night out, I was hoping they weren't expecting that from me.

It only took me five minutes to persuade my parents. They'd never done any sort of filming before, so they were obviously nervous about talking on camera. Not knowing what questions my parents would be asked worried me. I made it clear to them; 'Don't embarrass me!'

Chapter Seven

The following morning, George turned up at my door with one of the runners, James. He wasn't joining us in Colombia, although he was helping while we were still in England. I'd only known George for a few days whilst we'd been in London, so inviting him into my house still felt slightly strange. I was nervous.

After finding out the crew were staying the night in a Manchester hotel, I knew I was in for a long day. George wanted to get started straight away but he still hadn't met my parents. I was worried it would be slightly awkward. I was still very uncomfortable talking about cocaine around them, so I didn't know where the conversation would go.

As we headed out of the door to jump in a taxi to Old Trafford my parents arrived back from shopping. It was perfect timing and meant that they couldn't be interviewed until later. The crew were really nice to my family and I was a little less nervous about them being interviewed, but I knew that my parents would be asked everything about me on camera and it was playing on my mind.

After a short journey we arrived at Old Trafford. Standing outside a Premier League football stadium with cameras in your face is a bit daunting. There were tourists knocking about everywhere. Filming in London with the other three felt a lot easier.

Ten minutes passed, and a crowd was beginning to circle. They must have thought I was a new signing for the club, and I was lapping it up. George was directing me to do all sorts of poses. The longer we stood there, the more people gathered.

After thirty minutes of embarrassment, we headed back to my house. It was time for my parents to be interviewed - the part of the day that I was dreading. I had hardly had any time to discuss with them what I'd be happy with them saying on camera, so I was a little anxious. I knew they'd question them about me going to Colombia, but I had a feeling they'd go a little deeper.

With it being a rare sunny day in Manchester, George decided to do the interview outside. I got the feeling he chose to do that so that I couldn't hear what they were asking my parents. I ran upstairs to the back windows and stuck my head out. I couldn't hear a word, I was fuming!

My parents had an idea that I was involved with the documentary because I'd taken cocaine, but during the interview, my Dad said that he'd only just found out at the time of them asking him on camera, which was incredibly awkward.

If my Dad was a bit annoyed by it, you can imagine that my Mum was in total shock. She's totally against any drugs, so she was mortified to know that I'd done cocaine. There are loads of people who've done it. It's hard to explain, but we're in that generation where you grow up around it. She'd been brought up in a society where it's not really accepted or talked about.

Whilst the crew was busy interrogating my parents, I thought it would be a good idea to call one of my mates who was joining me on the night out. A lot of my friends seemed to know briefly what the show was about, but I think they were more interested in a free night out and getting their faces on TV.

Thirty minutes passed. There was still no sign of my parents. Again, I looked out of the window. They were still filming. I'd had enough of waiting so I went outside to listen in. As I walked out the patio doors into the garden, I could see in my Mum's eyes that she was finding it hard. My dad looked quite chilled out. He had a bit of sweat on his head but not too much.

I overheard the question; 'How do you think Louis will deal with criminals in Colombia?'

My mum responded with possibly the worst thing I could have ever imagined. 'Oh, I think he'll be a bit of a shit bag. He watches Crimewatch with a cushion and hates thunder.'

I had to butt in! 'Bullshit.' I couldn't believe what she had said!

That turned out to be the last question. I rushed around the house to find my Mum. I was fuming; 'Why have you just told a load of lies?'

She laughed. 'Well don't lie to me about the kind of shows you're going on!'

She'd got me back for telling her a white lie for several years by embarrassing me on national television.

Somehow, it was seven o'clock. The two scenes we'd filmed had taken around six hours! After filming in London for three days, I was knackered. It must have been the first time I wasn't looking forward to a night out in my hometown.

Even while I was hanging around mugging up to the camera at Old Trafford, I thought my mates might turn up drunk for our night out, and I wasn't wrong. I had some catching up to do, so I started on the vodka. Because they had been out drinking all day, I'd been expecting a call telling me they were too pissed to turn up. I hadn't got that call, so filming was going ahead.

None of the boys had done any filming before, so when they arrived at my house George told everyone to act as if the cameras weren't there. That turned out to be a bad idea as every single one of us started loudly shouting over each other. At one point, the crew had to take five minutes out while we settled down.

After drinking a few more pints to settle the nerves, we found ourselves standing in a circle shouting at each other about the football. It felt a bit strange that we had two cameras stuck in our faces with no music on. Usually if we'd be pre-drinking at my house then the music would be blasting. For legal reasons and copyright reasons, that wasn't allowed. The banter was the beat of the evening and it turned into a party without music.

As the night went on the smokers of the group made the decision to stand outside. With the crew hardly getting any footage, it gave them a good opportunity to question the lads. George wasn't shy with the questions.

'So, lads, what do you think of Louis going to Colombia?'

Surprisingly all of them had good responses. I expected a daft answer off one of them but that wasn't the case. They did me proud! The crew seemed happy, so it was time to head out to party properly in Manchester.

As we pulled up outside the nightclub, the crew thought it would be a good idea to jump out of the taxi and film us walking in. We'd all had a bit too much to drink so that was a challenge in itself. After three attempts at trying to walk in a straight line, we were eventually escorted to the VIP area of the club.

With the spirits and mixers flowing around the table, I thought it would be a good idea to make my way over to the dancefloor and start popping out some moves. As soon as the camera turned to me, I knew it was a bad idea. Seeing that on screen is something I can't wait to do, between my fingers from behind the sofa.

A while later, the crew left the club. Not that I can remember. It was another heavy night that ended mysteriously for me. I received a text message from George the following morning:

'So how was the night after we left you?'

I replied in a daze: 'I don't remember much to be honest. I'm guessing it went well because I'm at home!'

I wouldn't be for much longer.

Chapter Eight

Filming was over until Colombia. The next time I'd see the crew was on the day of departure in London. It was the first time I'd finally felt positive about doing the show. Meeting and spending time with the crew and other contributors made everything that little bit easier.

It had felt like there were a few hiccups along the way but nothing too much to put me off going. I had just over two days to pack, gather my final thoughts and prepare for the adventure of a lifetime.

With the two spare days, I went for a drink with my mates and discussed going to Colombia. They couldn't wait to see me on screen, tackling a hard subject in my way. I also spent a lot of those two days talking with my family. They didn't want me to come across badly and I left in high spirits, but under no doubt that I needed to represent them in a good way.

The day had come. It was 9am and I was on the train to London packed with commuters. But I wasn't heading to a 9-5 job like most people. I was on my way to Colombia, a country I associated with murder, drugs and dirty money. I remember feeling more excited than nervous. I think it was more the fear of the unknown. Anything could go wrong.

I received an email earlier that morning explaining the plan for the day:

'When you arrive in London you will be given a briefing by our safety officer. He will tell you everything you need to know before travelling. He will also take any questions you have in relation to safety or anything you may be concerned about. A first-aid kit and all equipment will be provided later today.' Brilliant, just what I needed to settle the nerves.

Looking out the windows of the train was making me wonder what Colombia would look like. Would everywhere suffer from poverty? Would some places be spectacular? Would they even have trains?

I'd been told not to do any research on the country before we got there, so I had literally no clue what to expect. The furthest I'd flown before was a four-hour flight to Tenerife, so for someone who hadn't really travelled outside Europe it was a real chance to see what life was like on the other side of the world. The trip was obviously going to be a real eye-opener. I still couldn't fully work out why I was chosen, and it all felt too good to be true.

Thirty minutes into the train journey, my head was all over the place. I remember thinking 'What the fuck is going on?' I was hours away from leaving the UK and It was the first time I'd really thought about the dangerous situations I could be put in.

I didn't realise how dangerous.

Travelling around London is never easy. Too many tube lines, too many trains and too many people. I'd worked out I was only four stops away from the production office, so I reluctantly jumped on the tube.

I heard an announcement over the Tannoy, 'The next stop will be Seven Sisters.' It was my stop. I panicked. The nerves started to kick in again.

After turning a five-minute walk in to a twenty-minute walk, I'd finally arrived at the production office and was greeted by Marc.

'Hi Louis, you made it. Come in and take a seat. Chanel, Troi and Amber will be arriving shortly. As soon as they do, we'll start the safety briefing.'

I couldn't believe how much work goes on behind the scenes. It reminded me of the start of the movie *Home Alone*. People were running around packing cases and camera equipment was being passed left, right and centre. There was no sign of George and James who'd been filming in Manchester with me.

A few minutes later, Amber arrived, followed by Chanel and Troi. Troi looked cool as ever, Chanel looked as crazy as the first time I met her, and Amber looked like she meant business. No change there then. Everyone seemed to be upbeat, but I could feel the nerves in the air. I don't think any one of us could quite believe we were about to fly to Colombia.

Marc walked over to the seating area and introduced us to Derek, who was going to give us the safety briefing. He looked like someone who you wouldn't want to meet in a back alley. Six-foot-tall and about four wide, Derek was from Liverpool, just thirty miles away from the city that Manchester scraps with the most, and not just in terms of the football teams. I reminded myself that staying on people's good side was one of my strengths.

'You alright mate?' I asked him.

'Yeah, now let's get a move on as there's a lot to cover.' I got the vibe this guy wasn't taking any shit!

As we walked across the office into the briefing room, Derek spoke up. 'Please take a seat and listen very carefully. This is a very important subject. If you miss anything it could be costly.'

I looked around the table to see the awe in everyone's face, my own look mimicking the expressions I could see on the faces around me in Amber, Chanel and Troi. It was at this point that I knew it wasn't going to be a sun, sea and sangria reality TV programme.

Derek introduced himself as an ex-army expert on hostile situations who had worked in war zones across the world, not only with the military, but with TV broadcasters from the UK to the Middle East, from BBC to Aljazeera. He then started to show us a PowerPoint presentation.

Usually I'd switch off straight away in a classroom environment but there was no chance of that. My eyes were glued to the projector screen. The PowerPoint started out quite briefly, advising us of the things to look out for whilst in Colombia. Interestingly, he told us the most likely incident we'd come across would be a car crash. I couldn't work out if he was joking or not.

'This is the bit where I need your full focus. If I told you there was no risk of kidnap or robbery, then I wouldn't be doing my job correctly. The main things you need to remember are always to listen and stay with the fixer. Never leave the hotel alone and never carry expensive valuables around with you.'

None of us had a clue what a fixer was, so Troi decided to ask.

'A fixer is the person who makes the arrangements. He will be the guy who knows the area very well. He may also be your translator whilst in Colombia. The crew will know a little more about that.'

I was guessing he was the man with the contacts. The questions started to fire around the room.

'Are we going to be safe?'

'What should we do in an emergency?'

These were obviously questions that he'd had aimed at him before because he was quick to reply. Then someone piped up, 'What happens if someone gets shot?'

He said, 'I'll show you now.'

After Derek demonstrated briefly to the team, I found myself wrapping a tourniquet around Amber's arm. I couldn't believe I was being taught how to deal with a bullet wound whilst filming a TV documentary.

Each one of us were given a safety kit containing medication, mosquito nets, a door stop, and a variety of other things. We were also given a small safety book containing essential information we made need in an emergency.

Despite the thoroughness of the briefing, there were still a few things I was unsure about. Would there be security with us? Would the people we interview be armed? With the camera crew following us around at all times, there was no way of us being discreet.

After several questions, Derek confirmed that there would be security joining us. I got the feeling that security didn't matter by the way he answered, but it was a little reassuring knowing they would be there. We all like to know where the emergency exits are on a Boeing 747, don't we, even if we'd have our heads between our knees praying if a plane ever went down.

We'd also been told that the crew would carry trackers in case of an emergency. So at least they'd be able to find me if I was kidnapped in Colombia.

There was only a small team of us going. The four presenters, two directors, a cameraman and a soundman. It was a skeleton team, really, in TV terms.

As we headed out the office doors to grab some lunch, we bumped into the cameraman and soundman. It was the first time all the cast and crew were finally together. Everyone introduced themselves. It felt like I'd started a new job, only we were about to travel to one of the most dangerous places in the world.

After arriving back from lunch, it was time to sit down with the whole team to discuss the first few days of Colombia. This was the bit I'd been waiting for. All eyes were on Marc.

'Ok guys, the first night we arrive we are hoping to film in the bars and clubs in Medellín centre.'

Everyone's eyes lit up. I wasn't expecting a night out as soon as we'd arrived.

'There is a 'but,' added Marc. 'Two of you will head out with the police on patrol. The other pair will be on the other side of the law finding out who is selling what and how much.' He told us under strict instruction, not to buy or take any cocaine ourselves.

With it being the first day I wasn't too bothered about the plan. I just wanted to get there safely. Just as the meeting was about to end, Marc confirmed the pairings.

'Amber and Troi, you will be out on patrol with the police. Louis and Chanel, you will be checking out the nightlife. This isn't an excuse to get drunk as soon as we arrive.'

At first, I thought I'd drawn the short straw but then realised, what better way to start the trip off than a night out in Medellín? If someone would have said to me at the start of the process that I'd fly to Colombia, test out the nightlife and come back, I would have taken the opportunity straight away.

Troi asked me what I thought of the schedule. I was still in shock. If the plan was to meet up with the local police and nightclub clientele on the first night, I was excited for the weeks ahead.

After a thirty-minute trip across London we'd arrived at the airport. There was no going back! I expected a short delay at check-in and security, I just didn't expect a wait of two hours! Knowing I would be flying over eleven hours on an aisle seat frustrated me even more.

As we made our way to the gate, Chanel revealed her seat number: 22A.

The seat to the right of me.

I knew there was no chance of sleeping on the flight, but then, how could I anyway? The second we sat down in the waiting area; the airport staff called for boarding. I couldn't believe it.

I was about to get on a flight to Colombia.

Chapter Nine

It was only a few minutes later that I was in my seat on the plane, getting strange looks from all around me. Most of the passengers seemed to be flying home from visiting the U.K. We were doing the complete opposite and we stood out.

I was pleasantly surprised by the legroom, but I couldn't say the same about the in-flight meal that I was handed two hours later. I'd rather have eaten the container in which it arrived. I turned to Chanel in disgust.

'If the food is anything like this in Colombia then I'm fucked.' She couldn't stop laughing. Aside from the food, the rest of the flight was uneventful, and we touched down in Bogota, the capital of Colombia, twelve hours later. We had slept a little, but I was still tired and hungry. As we stepped off the plane onto the airbridge I couldn't help but notice the dark, brooding clouds above. I was hoping they weren't setting the scene for the rest of the trip.

I had a gut feeling as soon as we entered the terminal that we would get stopped by security. As we headed through to passport control there were guards everywhere. It was as if they knew we were coming. Apart from the odd strange look, I managed to get through with no issues. It was just a shame I couldn't say the same about the crew and Chanel, who were stopped at customs leaving Troi, Amber and me waiting around. I hoped they hadn't stopped Chanel because of her looks, but any worries I had about them racial profiling us disappeared when I found out that they'd also stopped the crew. All the equipment had to be checked and it took some time to make sure everyone - and just as importantly, everything - safely escaped security.

After thirty minutes, it was time to make our way to domestic departures ready for another flight to Medellín. Walking through Bogota airport was a twenty-minute mission. Surprisingly, it was a modern and huge airport. I'd expected it to be a much smaller, shabbier place. As I looked around at the apparent luxury, I couldn't help but wonder how much the cocaine trade helped towards building it.

Shortly after arriving at the boarding gate, it was time for our second flight of the day, and after again taking my aisle seat, George shouted over to Chanel and me.

'Can you take a few videos of yourselves whilst on the flight? We might use them in the documentary.'

It was the last thing I wanted to be doing after such a long journey, but I knew it was only going to be the start of a very long trip, so we began filming, describing our feelings as we made the journey across Colombia.

After fourteen-hours travelling, we finally arrived in Medellín at seven in the morning. I knew that there was no going back! I had the same feeling of excitement when I'd landed in Magaluf, for my first lads' holiday, except that I knew this trip was going to be the complete opposite!

George informed us that Johnny would be meeting us at Arrivals, along with the fixer and driver. Johnny had been in Medellín for a week prior to our arrival, organising and researching for the show.

After collecting my bags from the luggage belt, I made my way outside. It was my first time stepping out on Colombian soil. I couldn't believe the humidity, which hit me like I'd walked into a sauna. There stood Johnny, who looked happy to see us arrive safely.

'Hey guys, nice to see you. How are you all? This is the transport we'll be using while we're in Colombia. The driver will take your luggage, but before that we need to film you guys arriving.'

We'd only been in Colombia five minutes and the filming had already started. Trying to look happy after a fourteen-hour trip was difficult, especially after being asked to repeat it four times. But that's reality TV. It's reality, repeated. If a moment is there to be captured, then it needs to be done right. And just like on other reality shows, where a Director might want to film something from another angle, Johnny and George didn't want to miss a thing. They needed as much footage as they could get over the next fortnight. They wouldn't be able to leave the editing suite to film what are called 'pick-ups' - it would be another fourteen hours of flights back to our filming location. Everything needed to be done there and then.

There was still no sign of the fixer. The driver took our luggage, all twenty-four bags of it, and packed it into the boot. After jumping on the coach, I spotted a guy at the front speaking with George and Johnny. He looked quite important.

Two minutes later, Johnny turned to the back of the coach.

'Guys, can you listen up a minute? This is Oliver, he is our local fixer. Obviously, you all know I have been in Medellín over the past week doing my best with him to secure the best interviews.'

I looked to Chanel, who was sat opposite me. 'This sounds like the guy Derek mentioned in the safety briefing.' She rolled her eyes as if to say 'obviously'.

'Hi, I'm Oliver. Nice to meet you guys, I will be looking after you whilst in Colombia. It is very important you always listen to me. There are three rules I would like you to follow. Never leave the hotel alone, never carry valuables around with you and never leave my eyesight without telling one of the crew.' The rules sounded very similar to the ones we were told in London by the safety officer.

I couldn't quite work out his accent. He definitely wasn't Colombian. I had to ask... 'Oliver, where is it you're from? I can't quite work out your accent?'

He chuckled, 'I was born in Germany, but I moved to Colombia just under twenty years ago.'

I wondered why he'd moved to Colombia in the first place, but it wasn't the time for questions - there would be plenty of opportunities for that during our trip as interviews would make up the bulk of what we'd be doing.

As we left the airport, the views took my breath away. Looking out of the coach windows, it reminded me of when I was on the train to London contemplating what everywhere would look like. I was expecting to leave the airport to see coca plants left, right and centre, but it was nothing like that. It looked and felt more like a Spanish village. Everywhere I looked there were mountains and greenery.

After travelling for forty minutes we hit heavy traffic, and the reason was obvious. It was the very thing that Derek the safety officer told us we were likely to come across - a car crash. I noticed a police car drive straight past the accident without even attempting to stop. It all seemed very normal as if it happens hourly. There seemed to be no rules on the road.

With the hotel being located twenty minutes away in the city centre I knew we weren't arriving anytime soon, so I decided to put my head down for a while. With the sun blazing down, I drifted off in and out of an erratic sleep.

Chapter Ten

I suddenly awoke to Troi shouting into my ear as the coach pulled up at the hotel; 'We are here!' As I stumbled out into the relentless heat, I noticed a plaque engraved onto the side door of the coach. It said, 'Medellín has left Pablo Escobar in the past and now he is evolving, growing in values and living for you'.

Fairly obviously, Medellín was his hometown. I just couldn't work out if the message meant they were for or against him? Well, I certainly had the time to find out.

I was surprised by the hotel, which was far nicer than I had expected. It may have been small, but it was very clean. All the staff was really friendly, referring to us as 'Sir' or 'Madam'.

Having only been in Medellín for one hour, it was too early to judge, but it just didn't feel like a city that used to be the murder capital of the world. After checking in, I headed upstairs to my room. It was the first time I'd been alone in twenty-four hours and it felt like I finally had some time to think and let things settle in. Well I thought it was until I heard 'BANG!'

It was George. 'Louis, can you make your way to reception as soon as you've got changed.'

I wanted to tell him to fuck off, but then I remembered I was there to film a TV documentary, not on holiday. It's hard not to feel like you're having a break when you arrive with your luggage in a foreign country.

After ten minutes laying on my bed feeling sorry for myself, I headed down to reception. Troi and me were first down followed by Amber and Chanel a few minutes later.

You could see in everyone's eyes that the jet lag had already kicked in. There wasn't much chat around the table. Johnny had told us the plan for the day, and we'd all listened. We were utterly reliant on Johnny and George to guide us through the next fortnight, and certainly on day one, nobody was stepping out of line.

'I thought it would be a good idea for you to head out with Oliver to Medellín Square, to get to know the area a little better' said Johnny. 'With it being the first day it's going to be nice and chilled out. If you have any questions about the city or anything else, Oliver's your man.'

Just as we were about to head out, Oliver introduced us to a gentleman. His name was Ivan and he didn't speak a word of English. He certainly looked like someone you wouldn't fuck with. Tall, broad and looking like someone we were better off with on our team, he towered over us, but was a gentle giant.

'Ivan will be joining the team whilst in Colombia. He will be our security. He is ex-special forces and knows the area very well.'

Knowing security would be watching us at all times felt slightly comforting. Even though my first impressions of Colombia were great, I still had worries in the back of my head about what might happen.

After walking ten minutes, we arrived at Medellín Square. The place was packed with market stalls, bars, clubs and restaurants. It certainly looked like the place to go for the nightlife. Music was blasting out, and it wasn't even midday. Oliver started to point out the names of the different places. I was getting the vibe that he was really clued up on the area.

Medellín Square was very similar to any square you might go to when abroad with your mates. The place was packed with tourists, which I was quite shocked to see. I hadn't expected Colombia's 'City of Eternal Spring' to be so popular, if only because it was in the mountainous area in the West of the country.

At night, British and American tourists as well as people from Germany and all over the world would populate the square itself. There was a small park area in the centre, which I pointed out to Oliver. He told us that the local street dealers hang around there. I couldn't see any but that was probably because it was mid-morning. I'd naively expected a dealer on every corner.

With the plane food turning out to be disgusting, we were all starving and eager to try out our first Colombian meal. I spotted a burger bar whilst strolling around the square.

'Shall we try that place?'

Everyone seemed happy enough, so we headed into the restaurant. Again, the staff seemed almost overly friendly. I'd only been in Colombia a few hours and I was already laughing with the waiter at my attempt at Spanish. As I sat down at the table, I thought it would be a good time to get to know Oliver a little better, especially since he'd be staying with us for the duration of the trip.

'Have you done much work like this before?'

'Yes,' he replied. 'I've been involved in many TV projects. I've worked with some of the top presenters in the UK. I won't name any names, but two of them are very famous in Britain. I will give you a clue though. One is known as a top chef and the other was known for his acting.'

It must have taken me around two minutes to work out who they were. It was becoming clear that he was highly experienced as a fixer. After chatting for a while, I was getting the impression that he was the man with the contacts. The in-between man I suppose.

With the conversation flowing, Oliver opened up about how he'd had a meeting in the restaurant we were eating in with one of Colombia's most famous hitmen, 'Popeye'. He'd worked on a previous show with him and, apparently, knew him well. I'd read about 'Popeye' previously. He was one of Pablo Escobar's personal hitmen. It felt a little crazy that I was sitting there eating with someone who had those kinds of contacts in his phone's address book.

Oliver noticed me looking out of the corner of my eye at Ivan. 'You guys are safe here. This is a very touristy area of Medellín.'

Even though I felt completely safe, having someone there on the lookout gave me some reassurance that everything was going to be cool.

There seemed to be a good vibe in the air. The food was good, and the drinks certainly went down well. All too quickly, it was time to head back to the hotel, get our heads down for an hour and get ready for the evening.

Without knowing how long I was staying in Medellín, I felt it unnecessary to unpack. Being a lad, I thought it was a good idea to live out of the suitcase, but fifteen minutes later my room looked like the cartels had come in and turned it upside down. I quickly showered and before I had the chance to rest, there was a WhatsApp message from the crew.

'Hi All, hope you had a good day out seeing the city with Oliver. Unfortunately, tonight's filming with the police has been postponed. Filming will continue tomorrow so you are free to do as you like tonight. Call time tomorrow will be 7am at reception. You will be briefed further in the morning. Have a good night!'

When filming is cancelled, you're thinking that it won't bode well for the show. The police excursion being cancelled upon arrival had me concerned that the programme would see us waiting around more than in action. There's a pressure to the process, and the thought has always been in the back of my head whenever I'm on television - is anything going to go wrong?

During filming, it was clear how important the show was to Johnny and George - they wanted to put the programme up for awards and even pitch to Netflix. That needs some of the edgier projects to come off for it to happen, so little stumbling blocks can add up to large frustrations. It's hard to schedule events at late notice in foreign countries, especially with criminals.

On a reality TV show, it's common to spend much of your time during the show talking about what you've got coming up next, but one person who lived in the moment was Troi. Clearly the youngest of the group, he had no fear about travelling and life in another country or culture. He just went with it. His family wasn't bothered about him doing cocaine, so he was quite chilled out about it all. He brought that element to the group - a relaxed, inquisitive attitude to the world.

I felt a bit like a big brother to Troi, and I think everyone felt similar. Johnny, in particular, took a shine to him and took him under his wing from the off.

In previous reality shows I'd been set up for pieces, but Johnny and George knew what I'd done in the past and played on it. There was a maturity to our interviews; they let my own questions come across unedited. You're conscious about why you've been picked to be part of the group and as I dozed off that night, I was very conscious of myself and living up to the perception that had got me on the plane in the first place.

Chapter Eleven

The next morning, I woke up feeling considerably fresher. Not knowing the plan for the day made it slightly easier to get up. I was excited for what was ahead. I threw on a pair of shorts and a t-shirt and headed downstairs to breakfast.

As I walked outside to the dining area, I was shocked to see the whole team already eating. Troi, Amber and Chanel were on one table and the crew sat on another. I was expecting to be the first down.

Chanel shouted, 'Morning Louis, how are you feeling?'

I just looked and laughed 'Yeah all good'. Everyone seemed to be eating either egg or fruit. I was a little confused, 'Has anyone got a menu?'

Everyone looked at me funnily. Amber giggled. 'There is no menu, Lou.'

I started laughing sarcastically. 'You've got to be joking! I hate egg and I'm not exactly going to survive on fruit.' There was no way I was filming a full day without any breakfast. I decided to take it upon myself to call the waiter over.

'Hi, would it be possible to order a bacon or sausage sandwich?'

The waiter looked at me as if he was saying the Spanish for 'what the fuck?' in his head.

With Oliver luckily speaking fluent Spanish I asked him to order me something. He looked to the waiter.

'El Tocino Y pan gracias.'

Ten minutes passed, and I was still waiting on my breakfast. For all I knew, he'd just asked for a mango omelette. While I concerned myself with the impending mystery food, George briefed us on the plan for the day.

'Today we will be visiting a favela just outside of Medellín. We will be meeting a social worker named Oscar. He is very well respected in the area, but this is the first place we will be going which could be very dangerous.'

Troi piped up. 'Wait, what's a favela?'

'A favela is basically another word for a slum. The ride is about forty minutes on the coach, so after breakfast, gather your belongings and meet back down at reception.'

Would we be meeting the social worker to see some of his work or was he some sort of ex-gangster who's saying he's changed his life around by helping the community?

When you're filming, producers and directors like to leave you guessing these imponderables - it makes for great TV, because the viewer then gets to see you react exactly how they would. It's fun... when you're on the other side of the screen.

I didn't even have time to think before the waiter came over with my breakfast. It was a slice of ham and one piece of stale bread. Not quite a bacon sandwich, but it was good enough.

After the not so lovely ham sandwich, I headed back to my room. I wasn't sure what I really needed for the day. What do you wear when you're going to a slum? There was no way I was turning up in my Gucci trainers and Louis Vuitton sunglasses. I remembered Ivan's words to us all.

'Never walk around in valuables.' I opted for the two plainest things in my suitcase, a pair of black shorts and a black t-shirt.

With it being the first time leaving the vicinity of the hotel, imagining where we were going was almost impossible. The picture I had in my head was somewhere with plenty of metal roofed houses crammed together and gang members hanging around the streets. But surely meeting a social worker wasn't going to be that dangerous?

Shortly after meeting back downstairs it was time to head out. It was the first day of filming in Colombia. With everywhere around the hotel being modern and touristy, going to a so-called slum felt slightly unnerving, but it was also part of the real Colombia we were there to discover. It was the reason we were being filmed, and it was what viewers would be hoping to see - the underbelly of the beast.

I think the four of us were still slightly confused about the plan for the day. Amber asked the crew for more info.

'Oscar, who you will be meeting, works very closely with local children, helping them in the community. This can be anything from studying, to helping them stay out of the gangs. Your aim for the day is to get to know a bit more about the neighbourhood, meet the kids and see what life is like for these people living in the area.' Said George.

I was buzzing. I had the chance to go somewhere where nobody would usually have access. I felt privileged. As we headed out of the city centre you noticed within five minutes the change in wealth. Buildings started looking shabby, considerably more people were homeless and there was a noticeably smaller police presence.

It was the first time I'd seen real poverty since arriving in Colombia. Looking out of the coach windows knowing we were heading to one of the neighbourhoods which is known for drugs and crime gave the trip much less of the holiday feel than the ride we'd taken from the airport to the hotel the day before. Despite being told Oscar was well respected in the area I knew, in the back of my head, all it would take was one nutter and we'd be in big trouble.

Twenty minutes later, we'd reached the rendezvous point - a busy area of Medellín just outside the indoor market. It was certainly not a place I thought we'd be meeting the very first interviewee. It was packed full of people shopping!

The crew quickly jumped out of the coach and started to unpack their camera equipment leaving Chanel, Amber, Troi and me sitting there. It was becoming obvious that this was going to be the meeting point for Oscar.

Seconds later the director opened the coach door, 'Ok guys, Oscar will be here in the next few minutes. Once you get out, I'd like you to introduce yourselves and after that I will direct you.'

Everything suddenly felt a bit dodgy. Sitting in the coach, in 30c heat, waiting for someone I'd never met before felt weird to say the least.

George informed us that Oscar didn't speak a word of English, so Oliver the fixer would be translating. It was a new thing for us all. I knew speaking through a translator on camera would be a tough ask, though it was the last of my worries. We were told to listen to the translator and look at the interviewee.

Eventually we got the nod. It was time to get out of the coach and meet Oscar. We walked a few yards towards the entrance of the indoor market and stood in a circle waiting for him. We had not been given a picture or description of him so spotting him was slightly difficult.

Two minutes passed and there was still no sign of him. Locals started to gather from all angles. People on mobiles were taking pictures of us. I had a feeling he was going to let us down.

Suddenly, I noticed a man walking towards us. He had long brunette hair and was wearing a red and black chequered long sleeve shirt. He looked to be only in his late twenties. I turned to the others, 'Surely that's not him?'

It was. It certainly wasn't the picture I had in my head. Maybe I just had that perception that everyone I was going to meet would look like a 'typical gangster' - bald head, muscly as fuck and tattoos everywhere. That certainly wasn't the case. He could have passed right by us and I wouldn't have even noticed him.

The little English he did speak helped massively. 'Hi, I'm Oscar, how are you?'

Chapter Twelve

After the four of us said our hellos, a bigger crowd started to gather. I suppose they weren't used to a bunch of strangers with a camera crew filming in the middle of their town centre. Then the director asked us to retake the opening shot of us meeting Oscar again.

It felt slightly surreal. I felt like I was some sort of movie star shooting a film. People were taking pictures of the second take, asking the crew what we were filming. I think Oscar was loving the attention too.

I turned to Oscar and said, 'Ha-ha your loving this aren't you?'

I then remembered that he didn't even speak English. I looked like a right dickhead!

Shortly after, Johnny informed us that we would be heading up to Oscar's neighbourhood. He wanted to show us the work he does within the community. Apparently, the vehicle we were using wasn't 'safe enough to go up to the favela' (how safe was safe enough?) so it would be our first time travelling on public transport. The bus journey was around one hour long.

With the bus stop only being ten minutes away, Johnny made the decision that we would walk. As we set off to the station through the busy town centre, the crew thought it would be a good idea to continue filming. It felt very surreal. When I'd watched documentaries in the past, I'd always found it strange that the presenters would be freely walking through a busy centre whilst filming. Doing it myself just felt mad.

As we continued walking side by side with Oscar, we reached the outdoor market. There must have been fifty plus market stalls set up along the street, most of them fruit stalls. Oscar decided to stop at one of them and tell us about the different types of fruits which are grown in Colombia.

The variety they had was crazy and some of them I'd never even heard of.

Amber shouted, 'Shall we try some local fruit?'

Me being a typical English tourist opted for an apple. I think Oscar looked slightly insulted that the other three were eating random fruits and I was munching on a Colombian Granny Smith.

The further we got down the street, the more attention we were getting from the locals, mostly from market workers offering us all sorts of shit. I think one of the workers even tried to sell me a hoover. I'm not sure if he just wanted me to stop filming, run over to the stall and then walk around Medellín centre with it, but unlike his wares, I was no sucker.

The further we walked away from the centre the quieter the streets became. We were filmed posing Oscar some questions we'd been itching to ask.

'So, Oscar,' said Troi, 'How did you end up in Medellín? How did you start at the community centre you are taking us to?'

'I came from a place outside Medellín, a rural area. In 1998, my family was forced to move due to conflict with the armed forces. We were placed in Comuna 13, an urban part of Medellín. They call this displacement. A few years later we were displaced again due to the Urban war. The place we are visiting today, Comuna 3, is where we managed to rebuild our lives. It is still the home of my parents and brothers. It's where I continue to do my community work. Medellín is split into six zones which are then divided into 16 communes.'

It seemed he'd had a real tough time but everything he was saying was with pride and a smile on his face. I felt slightly sorry for him, but I knew he didn't want that.

As soon as we arrived at the bus stop, I noticed one waiting to leave. This was the first time I'd seen any public transport since arriving. It must have been at least twenty years old, with no more than fifteen seats. I wasn't complaining though; it was all part of the experience. I expected to get on the bus and to be squashed in the corner - a bit like a busy London tube - but there wasn't one person on it! It felt a bit strange that it was the middle of the day on a busy afternoon and there wasn't one person heading to where we were going? Strange, and a little worrying.

As there was nobody on the bus, we were OK to continue filming. Oscar started to explain a bit more about what life is like in the favela. 'It's very hard to gain a good education, a decent job or even make enough money to survive.'

Despite the conversation being translated, everything he was saying seemed to be genuine, although it did make it slightly harder to feel the emotion he was showing. It was clearly a very personal thing to do for him to reveal his family history to four people who didn't know his language well, and who had never been to his country. Which of us could explain our country's quirks and nuances to a foreign stranger?

The further we got up the mountain towards the favela, everywhere started to look a bit more rural and unkept. There were barriers on almost every window, kids on motorbikes and now there was no sign of any police. The view looking down into the centre of Medellín was a treat in itself; we were travelling so high that you could see the whole city.

About thirty minutes into the trip the driver started to put his foot down. I wasn't sure if he was in a rush to get back down to the town centre or every bus journey was similar. I looked over to Troi who was sitting opposite, and he was literally hanging on to his seat for his life. Oscar started laughing - he was clearly used to getting flung about on the bus. God knows how the cameraman dealt with it!

As we got ever closer to the favela, I noticed the crew starting to put away their camera equipment, then everything got a bit more serious. I looked to Amber and her face reflected my own feelings. Without saying a word, we both knew what the other was thinking.

'Here we go.'

Chapter Thirteen

Oliver was holding forth as we headed deep into the favelas, climbing so high in altitude that even the air seemed quiet and thin. We held onto his every word.

'Ok guys, it is very important when we're in these types of areas that you DO NOT bump into anyone, DO NOT look at anybody for too long and finally if you have any issues direct them to Ivan or Oscar, who is obviously very well respected around the area.'

When we finally reached the top of the mountain, I was panicking as the bus pulled up. As I looked out the window, I could see the change instantly. The way people dressed, the way people looked and the way the buildings were painted and presented a completely different picture to the bustling market town of Medellín.

We were told to follow Oscar and Oliver off the bus and to head over to the local shop across the road. They said 'shop', but it was literally a house with metal barriers over it selling about four things.

I remember looking around and it was exactly how I'd imagined. When I'd seen films of slums on TV, with gangs hanging about on the street, metal roofs and a tension in the air, it wasn't so real. Being in the middle of that situation is very different. I was very conscious of how close everything and everyone was to the group. We all had the feeling that we were right in the middle of it.

We were told earlier in the day that the area was controlled by a gang. I could tell they'd been pre-warned otherwise there would have been trouble as soon as we stepped off the bus. There were tilted multi-storey houses all around, and behind each window there seemed to be someone staring at us. Their eyes felt like daggers in our backs.

Even children of seven were looking at us thinking, 'What are these people doing here?' From a young age, they'd probably been told to report back any strangers they see arrive in their village, and here we were, a large group of foreigners, capturing their homes on camera. It didn't feel like a place you would visit unexpectedly. Having the camera crew there made it slightly easier in a way. I mean, at least they knew who we were with..

Ivan and Oscar then led us to the shop across the road. It reminded me slightly of the video game Call of Duty. Everywhere felt so open, but fortunately for us, no-one was coming out of the undergrowth armed to the teeth. Oscar knew the owners of the shop. I thought he'd be scary, but he was well-liked and the nicest guy - he looked after all of us. Although Oscar wasn't a gangster type of guy I could still feel a slight atmosphere in the air.

Standing outside a shop in Manchester these days is enough for anyone, never mind standing outside a shop in the middle of a favela. Everyone was a little less loud, even Chanel.

Whilst the crew were discussing the next scene, I noticed three young lads walking over towards us. Here comes trouble, I thought. They only looked about fourteen, but I had a feeling that they'd been sent by someone from the area to check us out.

The smallest one of the group said to us in perfect English, 'Do you guys like football?'

That definitely wasn't the question I was expecting! I replied 'Of course, Manchester United?'

He said 'No, No, No! Real Madrid'.

I found myself in the middle of a slum having a chat with a fourteen-year-old about football. He seemed far too friendly. I was told earlier that day not to get too close to anyone, because you never know who they are. But football is a great conversation starter and it was amazing to bump into someone with such easy common ground.

Oscar walked over and smiled; he obviously knew them. I called over Oliver to translate. It turned out that one of them was Oscar's brother. They'd been waiting at the bus stop for us to come. I was shocked at how pleasant they were. Fourteen-year-old lads at home would have told us to fuck off by this point, but then, what can you do about City fans?

The director came over and explained what we would be shooting next. Oscar would be walking us through the streets of the favela, telling us a bit about the things he did for the area and generally showing us around.

After standing outside the shop for fifteen minutes, I noticed that the crew were getting slightly agitated. We were told in London by the safety officer to never stay in one place longer than necessary and Oliver clearly believed the time was right. 'Guys, I think it's time to make a move.'

Oscar started to walk down the street with the four of us at his side. There was so much to ask him. I just couldn't get used to speaking through the translator - interviewing someone whilst walking was a task in itself, especially walking through the streets of Colombia's equivalent of the ghetto.

As we started to walk further down the road, people were noticeably starting to gather on their balconies. Someone must have informed them. I'm not sure how but everyone seemed to come out in sequence. All eyes were on us!

Amber opened up the questions, 'Can you tell us a bit more about what you do for the community?'

'Yeah, I run the local youth centre. We do different activities and learning games throughout the day and try to give the kids the best education possible with the resources that are available to us.'

I had to ask the question I'd been waiting to ask since I arrived off the bus, 'How do people make enough money to live up here? From what I've seen there doesn't look to be many job opportunities?'

'Well that is a good question. People in this area can join a gang at an early age or they can try making money another way. Some even go into prostitution.'

I could see he was struggling to answer. Looking around you could see that there weren't many job opportunities. It was either join a gang or sell whatever you can to get by.

As the questions continued, it was becoming more and more obvious how much Oscar cared about the area and the people living there. I was really taken back by it all. I remember questioning myself - how can someone be forced out of their home on two occasions and still have the strength to continue fighting to help people?

More and more people started to gather on the streets. Considering we were in the middle of the so called 'ghetto', it was surprising how welcoming most people were to us being there, especially filming as we went. Obviously, Oscar was well-known around the area, which helped. I'm not sure it would have been the same to unwanted visitors!

We'd been on the street interviewing Oscar for around twenty minutes before we got the nod to wrap it up. It was time to head to Oscar's family home. He said it was only a five-minute walk around the corner. On route, Oscar was greeted by everyone he saw. I could tell that the people in the neighbourhood had a huge respect for him. It almost felt like he was a local celebrity.

Whilst he stopped to chat to one of the locals, I finally had some time to look up, breathe and take everything in. I felt like the last thirty minutes walking through the streets was just one big blur. I must have been buzzing on adrenaline. Even though we were in such a dangerous place, I was really enjoying it. It was becoming clear that Chanel, Troi, Amber and I weren't there just to explore the world of cocaine itself, but to see how it affects different people and areas.

As we were walking towards Oscar's house Chanel said, 'Can you hear that noise?' Troi responded, 'Yeah what an earth is that!?' The sound was getting louder the closer we got. None of us could quite work out exactly what it was.

I heard it again, only this time it was a lot closer.

Chapter Fourteen

As we passed an alleyway, I noticed two men standing there arguing. There were two cockerels going toe-to-toe in a fight! It looked like they were training them. This was the first time I'd seen something slightly disturbing since arriving in Colombia. I don't think anyone wanted to upset Oscar and ask why it was happening, so we carried on walking.

I remember thinking in the back of my head, 'Is everyone being super-friendly for the cameras?' Oscar didn't seem to blink an eye at what we'd seen. I'm not sure if it was legal in Colombia, but it definitely didn't sit right with me.

When we arrived at Oscar's house, we were greeted at the door by his parents. Again, they were so welcoming. I was really intrigued to see what one of the houses would look like from the inside.

We were invited in and the whole house was no bigger than a school classroom - in fact, getting the whole crew in as well as the four presenters was a struggle. Oscar's parents showed us around and it didn't take long. There was a front room with two beds in it, a small bedroom and a kitchen area. All the rooms were on the one floor. There was an instant respect for them. It was clear that their living conditions weren't great, but it didn't seem to bother them. They were so pleased to show us around.

As we stood around the kitchen table, I thought it would be a good opportunity to ask them a few questions. 'What do you think of Oscar's work and the things he does for the community?'

His mum replied, 'Oscar is an incredibly kind person. He puts a smile on my face when times are hard'. Again, I felt a sense of pity for them, but I knew they didn't want that.

Chanel then asked how they made enough money to survive. Oscar's dad seemed to be slightly camera shy, so his mother spoke again. 'We try and sell anything we can to get by.'

I felt a little helpless. Even though they were living in such poor conditions, they seemed happy enough with what they had. It made me think about what we take for granted, what we need to survive and what we don't need in order to get by in relative comfort back in Britain.

Time was flying. We'd already been in the favela over two hours and we hadn't reached the community centre yet. Johnny and Ivan informed us earlier in the day that we would have to leave no later than dusk for safety reasons. Time wasn't on our side.

Shortly after, we said our goodbyes to Oscar's parents and thanked them for inviting us to their home. Next up was the community centre.

The director told us that we might just have enough time to speak with the children involved and possibly play some activities with them. This was something I had been looking forward to since the morning. I wasn't sure what to expect. Surely it wasn't going to be like a youth centre back home?

During the walk everything Oscar's parents had said was playing on my mind. I think meeting and speaking to someone who was a little older made me think of my family. I couldn't imagine what it must have been like growing up there. Especially after twice being forced out of their homes.

After walking for a few minutes, we arrived at the community centre. It looked exactly how I had imagined. A small block building, pretty much in the centre of the favela painted in multi colours. At the side of it was a mini football pitch. I say football pitch, it was basically just a concrete ground with two broken nets.

Before we'd even walked through the door all the kids come running over to us. It put an instant smile on my face. They must have only been between five and fourteen and it was like they'd never seen people from outside the area before. They looked so happy to see us.

Oscar literally had to escort us through the door. Inside were a few tables and chairs, a blackboard and not much else. I stood at the front of the classroom and introduced myself, 'Hi, I'm Louis and I'm from Manchester'. When the translator repeated back what I said all of them looked shocked and I wasn't sure why.

One of the younger lads shouted, 'Manchester United!' I knew I'd have to chat with him if I had the chance. Chanel, Amber and Troi then introduced themselves. Due to the translation, twenty minutes had already passed by.

Shortly after we were asked by the director to split up into groups to do some activities. I shouted out 'OK, who wants to team up with me?' The kid who shouted out 'Manchester United' put his hand up, followed by a couple more. I felt a bit like a teacher at the time.

The four of us sat towards the back of the room in a circle. We'd been given some newspaper, glue and paint to make papier-mâché Halloween props. They'd obviously done it before because they knew what they were doing more than me. After ten minutes my arm was covered in paint. They decided to paint on me instead.

It was finally sinking in how lucky I was as a child. I remember moaning at the age of ten because I didn't have a mobile phone, yet they were sat there with some newspaper and paint and seemed just as happy.

Having nieces of a similar age back home made the whole trip to the community centre that bit more real. I was keen to find out what life was like for a youngster living in the favelas. 'So, what do you get up to when you're not at the community centre?'

At first, they looked reluctant to answer. They looked slightly confused. One of the girls finally responded. 'There isn't much to do, I just play'. I got the vibe that they didn't really want to speak to much.

With them being so young, I didn't want to put too much pressure on them. My next question was; 'Do you ever get scared?'

The two lads instantly said 'No, not really'.

I wasn't sure if that was a manly thing or they genuinely weren't scared. The girls on the other hand said 'Yes, sometimes it can be very scary'.

Chanel was sitting just in front of us with her group. I overheard her asking one of the children if they were looking forward to going trick or treating? I was surprised by the answer;

'We are not allowed to go out during the night, because we could get kidnapped.'

It was strange to hear a girl so young even being aware of what kidnapping was, and heart-breaking too. They were just children, but they lived in a very harsh, very adult world. Their innocence wasn't guaranteed - it had to be fiercely protected.

After washing all the paint off my arm, we headed outside. With the remaining time we had left at the community centre I wanted to make the most of it. I asked Oscar to ask the children if they wanted to play a game of football. Before he'd even finished the sentence, I had about thirty kids running around the pitch shouting for the ball.

Chapter Fifteen

Amber and Troi were asked to film another scene, which left Chanel and me entertaining the kids. It was nice to see them enjoying themselves. Chanel seemed to be teaching them some sort of handshake, whilst I was legging it around the football pitch. I was shattered! Playing in 30c heat was totally different to rainy Manchester. Once again, I got caught up in the moment and completely forgot we were filming a documentary.

Chanel and I were a little confused as to what Troi and Amber were doing. I asked the crew - 'They're filming a scene with some of the local teenagers.' said Johnny. I didn't ask any further, but I was keen to hear what they had to say. We'd already heard from Oscar's parents who were of the older generation, and we'd spoken to the children. Surely the teenagers would talk a little more about the favela? It was time to head inside.

We'd only been in the area for eight hours and I already felt a connection with everyone, but not long after, it was time to leave. I think the children were just as upset about us leaving as we were. I suppose it was something completely different to a normal day in a ghetto! I never thought I'd be sad to leave a place like that, but I was, and I felt like they were too. When you leave somewhere in the UK to travel home, you know that you might be back one day. But when you're making a once-in-a-lifetime trip to a small village, you know with a high degree of certainty that you'll never be back, never see those people again, it weighs heavily on you.

Before I was about to walk out the door, I called one of the kids over, the lad who shouted, 'Manchester United'. I said to him 'OK, you have to keep this quiet. Here are my sunglasses. They're for you.' It was priceless to see his face light up.

He smiled, put his finger to his lips and said, 'Thank you, sshhh!'

If I'd known the situation before arriving, I would have tried to bring every single one of them a gift. I remember thinking, if I ever get the chance one day to come back and surprise them, that I would. I had a picture in my head of going back and rebuilding their football pitch.

Suddenly it was getting dark. Ivan told us that it was time to leave. Knowing we had to walk back through the favela in dusk, I felt slightly on edge. Luckily, Oscar told us that he would join us on the bus back down to Medellín centre, which I was pleased about.

I was quite emotional walking back to the bus stop. Even though I'd only known the kids for a few hours, I was sad that I'd probably never see them again. As we left Oscar told us that seventy-five percent of the children we had met during the day, would end up in a gang. It was the last thing I wanted to hear. The children I'd just met certainly didn't feel like future gangsters.

As we walked through the streets of the favela towards the bus stop everywhere felt slightly more intimidating. I wasn't sure if it was because it was getting darker, but there was a different atmosphere in the air. It almost felt like it changed in an instant. I was getting the vibe that the locals didn't want us there any longer.

Oliver said, 'OK guys, stay together and try to speed up a little'.

We eventually got to the bus stop. The return bus looked a lot busier. Oscar seemed to work his magic and managed to get us on first. As the driver set off, I noticed a couple of the children who we'd seen at the community centre in the distance waving at us through the window. They must have followed us up to the top of the favela. It was only day two and my emotions were being tested already.

Before I even had time to wave back, the bus driver slammed his foot on the accelerator and drove off. I'd already learnt from the journey up the mountain that the bus drivers don't hang about! An hour drive took about thirty minutes. Before we knew it, we were back in Medellín centre. It was time to say goodbye to Oscar. As I stepped off the bus I said, 'Thank you for showing us around. Everything you seem to be doing is working. Keep up the good work and I wish you all the best'. It was at this point that I wished I spoke Spanish.

Again, he looked at me as if to say 'What'? I'd completely forgotten that we'd been speaking through a translator all day. Oliver passed the message on and away Oscar went.

That was the last we saw of him.

The day seemed like one big blur, and as we made our way back to the hotel, I remembered that Troi and Amber had interviewed the teenagers. I had to ask, 'Go on then, what did the guys from the favela have to say, the teenage lads?'

Troi responded - 'Wow, it was actually mad hearing from someone who's a similar age. One of their friends is apparently missing. He was on the run from a gang, but there not quite sure where he is, they said he could have been murdered!'

I looked to Troi 'Wow, you serious?
I thought everything was a bit too nice.' Finally, someone had admitted that there were still problems in the area with gangs. I was gutted that I wasn't in on the interview, but I suppose we couldn't all do everything.

Given that I'd just left one of Colombia's most dangerous neighbourhoods, I was calm. Surely everywhere we'd visit wouldn't be the same?

When we arrived back at the hotel the first thing on my mind was food. We were all told to meet back down at reception after thirty minutes to discuss eating options. I was so hungry that I didn't even bother going upstairs.

I noticed Oliver was sitting on his own outside, so I joined him.

'Well that was an interesting day wasn't it?'

'Yes, Louis, very. Things are about to get a lot more interesting.' His German accent made it that little more serious. I didn't exactly know what he meant by it, but I knew he wasn't going to tell me. The crew were keeping everything a secret as long as they could, that way everything would be as spontaneous as possible on camera.

Chapter Sixteen

After spending almost two full days with Oliver, I felt comfortable enough to ask him a few questions. I knew he'd lived in Colombia for nearly twenty years, but I just didn't quite get the role of his job. I knew it was the right time to ask. 'So, without sounding rude Oliver, what exactly is your job?'

He looked furious. 'I play a very important part in the production of the show. I get the access to locations, people and of course I'm your translator'.

I'd always wondered how presenters got access to criminals. I had my answer; it was people just like Oliver.

I didn't want to dig too deep in to why he'd moved to Colombia, but I was guessing it was that he'd met a Colombian woman. Why else would a German man move to Colombia? He went on to tell me a bit more about the history of the country. I'd never been a fan of history, yet he seemed to make it interesting.

Surely, he knew about the history of Pablo Escobar. I asked him 'Why is he so famous?'

He responded with something that really shocked me. – 'Pablo was nowhere near as big as the new drug cartels.'

He mentioned a guy named Antoniel Usuga, who apparently now runs a cartel bigger than Pablo ever did back in the day, The Cartel Del Golfo. He said, 'You will find out a lot more about them later in the trip'.

Surely, we weren't going to meet any of them, I thought.

I couldn't quite believe that there's still groups out there running cartels bigger than ever. It wasn't fact, but what he told me shortly after kind of proved it. 'Fifteen years ago, Colombia produced an average of five hundred tonnes of cocaine a year. Now it has risen to nine hundred tonnes'.

I was that deep into conversation that I'd completely forgotten that I'd not eaten. Minutes later, Chanel, Troi, Amber and the rest of the crew joined us downstairs.

Johnny said; 'Ok, whilst your all here I'd like to say a few things. Firstly, I want to thank you for a great day filming. Tomorrow is going to be a long day. I won't tell you exactly what we will be doing yet, but we need to be up and ready for 8am.'

Chanel called out whilst laughing, 'Now what's for tea?'

One of the crew said, 'Who wants a take-away?' Every single one of us ordered the biggest pizza on the menu and after such a long evening, it was just what we needed. Shortly after, it was time to head upstairs to bed

It had been an eye-opening few days to see how people live. Even the crew who'd seen it all before on screen and in their research, were blown away by being there and seeing it first-hand. From the point of view of the presenters, it had been an emotional rollercoaster. To hear that the kids would probably end up in gangs had affected us all. We just wished we could do something - nothing to do with television, but just in our own hearts to help.

I hadn't really known what to expect when I was asked to go on the trip. I left Manchester with a stupid attitude that everyone I would meet in Colombia would be a nasty fucker. That definitely wasn't the case. Everyone we'd met up to that point was friendly, welcoming and extremely open.

So far, so good.

Chapter Seventeen

The next morning, after a terrible night's sleep, I woke to an awful nightmare. I was being kidnapped!

When I opened my eyes, I had no idea where I was for a couple of seconds. Then it came back to me, with my location and the events of the day before gradually replaying in my mind. Colombia, Medellín, Oscar, the children, the goodbyes, the regret about leaving a different world behind up the mountain in the mist. There had been a lot of emotion, but we had almost no time to let it sink in.

It was the third day, it was 7:30am and the mental toll from what we'd filmed so far - as well as the jetlag - needed to be shaken off. We had another day's filming to prepare for, but first I called the one person we all do when we need a friendly word in our ears.

'Hi Mam. You OK?'

It was the first time I'd spoken to anyone back home since arriving in Colombia.

She replied, 'Is that you Lou?'

'Yeah, it's me, Mam. I've rang you off this same number for ten years now!' I laughed. 'The good news is, I'm still alive'.

'Don't be so daft', she said.

She wanted to know everything. The conversation almost felt like a Q&A and I couldn't blame her. I'd have been the same if I had a family member in Colombia. The first thing she thought to ask was if the hotel was clean!

Like any parent she probably didn't care too much at this point what I was up to, just more the fact that I was safe. I went on to tell her pretty much everything hour for hour what I'd been up to. Twenty minutes passed like five. I came off the call feeling incredibly grateful, not only for the position I was in, but it had hit me how lucky I was as a child, especially compared to the children we'd met the day before. The trip was becoming a real eye opener as to what life is like for the less fortunate.

Just as I was getting deep in thought, I received a WhatsApp message from Chanel. 'Fruit and egg on the breakfast menu, see you downstairs.'

I looked at my phone in disgust and replied. 'Shock! Great.' There was no way I fancied filming a full day again with no breakfast, but I knew I'd have to get used to it. I headed downstairs to the seating area. It was the kind of place we ate, drank and generally chilled out. It was pretty much the only place in the hotel where that was possible.

As I walked outside, Chanel was sat there laid back in the chair, cigarette in one hand, a piece of fruit in the other.

'Good sleep?'

'Not great, I just couldn't doze off'.

I told her about my nightmare. For some reason she started laughing, but that was typical Chanel. A few minutes later Troi and Amber joined us at the table. We still didn't know the plan for the day. There were rumours that we'd be heading to another favela.

Johnny came over to tell us.

'Morning guys, Good sleep?' Everyone nodded but me.

'Thank you again for yesterday, with everyone feeling the jet lag today should be a lot easier. We're heading to Comuna 13, another neighbourhood in the city. It's a very touristy part of Medellín with a lot of history so it should be a nice chilled day getting to know the area a little better.'

I couldn't understand how visiting a favela would be seen as a tourist attraction. I had to ask. 'What exactly do you mean by touristy?'

While Chanel, Troi and Amber laughed at my question, Johnny understood. 'There will most likely be groups visiting the area, possibly on Pablo Escobar tours.'

I looked to the other three, 'Wait, people actually visit there for tours?'

'Yes, it's a very popular area of Medellín. Oliver will explain a little more once we're on the coach ready to go.'

Troi was still a little confused, a bit like the rest of us. 'What is it exactly we're going to be doing?'

'We'd like you to mingle with some of the tourists and ask them a few questions. Why is it they're visiting? Have they been there before? Remember - we are here to discover about the cocaine industry, so you might want to question them on if they've been offered any whilst in Colombia.'

I couldn't work out why people would fly from all parts of the world to visit this place? Surely there was some serious history behind it? I shouted Oliver over who was sitting on the other table eating his breakfast.

'I'm a bit confused, Oliver. What's the history behind this neighbourhood? Why would people want to visit it as a tourist? Surely, it's too dangerous.'

Troi and Chanel nodded their heads in agreement. All of us looked to Oliver.

'Well, in the 1980's and 1990's, the neighbourhood was controlled by groups loyal to Pablo Escobar. After his death in 1993, other drug cartels sought control of the area, then in 2002 the Colombian military carried out an operation, Operation Orion, to take back control of the favela. Several people lost their lives which makes the neighbourhood special. It used to be the murder capital of the world. Now it's a lot safer to visit due to the changes in the area. I think you'll be very surprised when you see it.'

I thought we'd be just casually walking through a favela, like the day before, but as tourist. That obviously wasn't the case and it made a lot more sense. We were in Escobar country, and the history of the neighbourhood would make it a fascinating day. I couldn't wait to start.

The only thing I was concerned about was randomly walking up to strangers trying to engage in a conversation. If I was on holiday or travelling, I certainly wouldn't want to be speaking to four random British people with a camera crew. I suppose it was all part of getting used to being a so called 'presenter'. It made me think a lot about the process of reality television and my role within it.

I knew from the get-go when I took the job that our experiences in Colombia were going to be actual reality as opposed to what I'd been involved with in the past. A year earlier, I'd flown out to Greece to film a dating show. It was a hotel full of cameras where I was told to speak to the person I got on with the most. The cameras are just fixed on one spot. Directors and producers just watch from a screen area and spot out any potential storylines.

'Why don't you go and speak with that person?'.

In the back of your mind, you're wondering 'Why can't I go and chat about what I want to chat about, or is that not interesting enough?'

This was a completely different scenario. There were gangs around us in the street and it was completely different to what I've done in the past. I loved the change.

I got along with a few of the people I'd met on dating shows, but there were also times when I just wanted to go home. There was no time in Colombia when I felt that. It was all so intriguing and exciting. I could have done it for months and months.

By the time I'd eaten what breakfast I could find, it was time to leave. Oliver, Ivan and the crew were joining us. The trip was around a forty-minute drive. Everywhere we visited seemed to be about forty minutes away. It started to become a standing joke with the crew.

I ran upstairs quickly to get changed. As I walked through the door of my room, I noticed the safety kit we'd been given for the trip on the floor. There was a tourniquet hanging out. That was the equipment we were given to stop the blood from someone if they were shot!

I stopped and sat on my bed for a minute. Was I taking everything for granted? They'd obviously not given us the equipment as a joke. I'd not really thought about the seriousness of the trip until then. I had the feeling that we had been eased into our Colombian experience. Sure, it had started out with the easier interviews and trips, but towards the end we might get hit with the real stuff.

I didn't have a clue what was to come.

Chapter Eighteen

After a long, warm and sweaty coach trip, we finally arrived at Comuna 13, also known as San Javier. The entire town was a kaleidoscope of colour. Houses were piled up the street, what looked like hills constructed entirely out of people's homes. It was as if paints of every colour had been thrown at the town. As well as multicoloured houses, every surface seemed to be covered in graffiti. There were 100,000 people crammed together in San Javier, yet there seemed an innate sense of peace about the place.

We weren't on our own in visiting the town. There were tour guides everywhere. The female one that I noticed straight away had a camouflage bucket hat on. Attached to the side of it was a microphone and I could hear her yelling at the tourists from inside the coach. She sounded passionate about something; I just couldn't hear what.

We were advised to stay on the coach while the crew prepared the equipment. The heat inside was getting intense but luckily it was only ten minutes before George poked his head through the door.

'Ok, we're all set. When you get off the coach, we'd like you to make your way up the main street. As you can see there are several tour guides and hundreds of tourists here. I'm sure some of them are willing to have a chat with you lovely people.'

As I stepped off the coach into the scorching heat, Chanel said to me, 'Surely the tour guides aren't going to be happy with us just joining in. It's a bit random isn't it?'

One of the crew members overheard us talking.

'The tours are free, they won't bother.'

At the bottom of the long narrow road overlooking the favela was a row of shops. There was a barber shop, an ice-cream shop and a few others. If I didn't know it used to be one of the most dangerous neighbourhoods in Colombia, then it could have felt like a busy European street. There were people everywhere.

Whilst everyone was standing around discussing the scene, Chanel and I ran over the road to the ice-cream shop. There was no way I was missing out, especially after breakfast had consisted largely of fruit again. With the little Spanish I knew I managed to order us two vanilla cones.

As we made our way back across the road. I heard someone shouting:

'Louis, Chanel!' It was Ivan.

He looked pissed off. Running off without letting him know had not gone down well. Oliver walked over. We were in trouble.

'Guys, I know it's safe here, but you need to let us know if you're going to be leaving the group.' I felt like a naughty kid on a school trip.

As we set off walking up the long narrow road, it was only metres before we bumped in to the first group of tourists. Most of them looked European, some of them British. They were standing in front of the female tour guide I'd spotted as we arrived. The woman appeared to be shouting. I walked over slowly and casually joined the back of the group. With the cameras filming us from behind and a good fifty metres away, it just looked like I was a random guy joining in.

Whilst the tour guide continued yelling in Spanish all I could hear was hip-hop music being blasted from the houses above. I gathered that was the reason she was shouting; she was trying to be heard above the music. Chanel, Troi and Amber sneaked into the group, with me at the back.

Troi looked at me as if to say, 'What the fuck is she talking about?'

After five minutes of continental bellowing, she eventually translated into English.

'Many buildings and walls which you can see around you are full of graffiti; these are painted by a local artist.'

She told us how the government offered locals free paint and sprays to paint the neighbourhood different colours after the conflict ended. I was surprised at how good it looked, but then she went on to tell us that they hosted graffiti festivals each year where artists visited from all over South America.

The tour guide then walked our group to several different buildings, telling us the names of some of the more popular artists. Whilst most of the group was taking selfies in front of the street art, I noticed a guy standing alone. I was positive he was European. Knowing the crew wanted us to mingle I knew it was the right time to try and spark a conversation with someone.

'Hey mate, you ok?'

He looked at me in mild disgust.

'Que?' He didn't understand a word I'd just said.

I knew it was going to be hard trying to find someone who spoke English, never mind someone who was willing to speak on camera. We weren't getting much luck.

George called us over.

'It's important that you try and get speaking with some of the tourists.'

It was probably the first time I felt slightly annoyed with our directors. We were all clearly trying to engage in conversation, but people just weren't willing to talk. It was a bit of a Colombian stand-off, and Johnny and George were starting to get concerned about the lack of footage.

I had to try a new approach. All four of us were trying to chat, and I felt like it might be slightly intimidating for the tourist. I asked the directors if it was OK for the four of us to split up. Their response was; 'Listen Louis, it's a documentary, it's totally up to you how you want to do it.'

It was definitely the answer I was looking to hear. Even though there was little pressure, I felt like I was there to do a job, and we had a key role in making a good TV show.

I called Chanel over. 'Chanel! If you're happy with it, we'll split into two pairs. I think it might be a bit easier.'

She was happy to go along with the idea. Troi and Amber did the same and went off together as a pair.

A couple of minutes later, several people joined the group. Chanel and I looked at each other as if to say, 'They're ours!'

A young man joined in at the back. He looked like he was alone - the perfect candidate. Chanel and I walked over to him.

'Hello, do you speak English?' The anticipation waiting on an answer from him was unreal.

'Yes, I do. How can I help?'

We were in.

'Nice to meet you. Where is it you're from?'

'I'm from Central America. How about you guys?'. We finally found someone who was willing to interact. I wasn't sure at this point if he knew we were with the camera crew or we were just some random tourists.

I had to make him aware, well Chanel did; 'I know it's a bit random, but we're currently filming a TV documentary focusing on the cocaine industry. As you can see there are several cameras following us around. Are you willing to have a little chat with us on camera?' He looked scared shitless!

'Err I don't know about that guys. What is it you want to chat with me for?' It was time to win him over, using our British charm.

Chapter Nineteen

'You look like a confident person who isn't afraid to talk, so that's the reason we approached you. Basically, we're looking to speak to people from all over the world to find out their views on not just cocaine, but Colombia itself.'

That persuaded him. He looked slightly confused but he was happy to chat. I looked over my shoulder and Troi and Amber were already chatting with two young girls. They'd beaten us to it.

With the guide about to move to the next part of the tour, we only had a few minutes to interview the young man we'd just stopped.

'I've noticed you're alone. Are you travelling or do you live here?'

'Yes, I'm traveling. I've always wanted to come here. It's a beautiful country', he responded.

I remember thinking in the back of my head that surely there's another reason he's travelling alone to Colombia. Either for the partying, women or drugs. I guess that was because I'd never heard any of my friends or family say to me, 'I'm off to Colombia'. I mean, have you?

I'd have most likely responded, 'You're going fucking where?!'

It linked perfectly to my next question - 'Being British, travelling to Colombia alone would be seen as slightly risky. Do you feel safe over here?'

'I feel completely safe. I've been here two weeks and seen many cities. I was told if you stay in the places you are told to stay then you shouldn't have any issues.'

Chanel was keen to get to know what he'd been up to whilst in Colombia. 'With us currently filming we've not really had the chance to go out in Medellín yet. Have you managed to party since arriving?'

He glared at us - 'Guys! If you haven't been out in Medellín Square you need to. It's one of the best nights I've ever had'.

Johnny wanted us to dig a little deeper as to why. Was it because of the things I'd originally thought, drugs or women, or just the general nightlife?

The tour guide shouted 'OK, it's time to move on, if you can follow me'.

I knew there was little time, so I went in for the jugular.

'It's obvious that Colombia is well known for not only producing cocaine but also exporting it. Have you been offered any whilst here?'

He looked pissed off that I'd asked. 'I don't touch drugs. Not everyone who visits Colombia is here for the cocaine.'

The interview was flowing, and I felt like we'd gained enough rapport to ask him; 'So why exactly is it you've decided to visit here?'

'As I said a minute ago, Colombia is a beautiful country with beautiful women. What single man wouldn't want to?'

I laughed and nodded my head. 'Yeah, very true!'

We'd only been interviewing him for around five minutes, and I could already see he was getting frustrated. I had a feeling he thought we were typical journalists who were painting Colombia in a bad light. Or maybe he just wanted to focus on the tour?

I got the vibe that we weren't getting much more out of the interview and it was becoming clear that Colombia, especially Medellín, wasn't just about the cocaine industry. It was about so much more. After a few more questions we thanked him for speaking with us and moved on. As we walked off Chanel murmured, 'Wow, I thought everyone just comes over here to get on the coke.'

The director called us over - 'Good questions there, guys. I know it's hard trying to chat with people, especially because of the subject and the pressure of the cameras.

Amber and Troi are just finishing their chat and then we'll catch up with the tour guide. Hopefully she will show us the electric stairs.'

I looked up. 'Wait, what electric stairs?'

'You'll see shortly.'

As we approached the top of the hill, the music from the houses was getting louder and louder. Believe it or not the song playing was, 'Gangsta's Paradise'. Not the track I expected to be playing in what used to be one of the most dangerous neighbourhoods in Colombia. Quite a coincidence.

Whilst Troi and Amber were finishing their interview further down the street, Chanel and I thought it would be a good idea to try and catch up with the rest of the tour.

I wanted to know what the director meant by electric stairs. After power walking a little further, I spotted the stairs in the distance. They looked more like escalators than electric stairs, but that wasn't the issue. Why the fuck were they there?

Amber and Troi came running over. Troi shouted; 'Have we missed anything?' Amber spotted the stairs in the distance like me. 'What an earth is an escalator doing here?' George, as was often the way, gave us an explanation.

'Before I tell you, we'll stop at this shop and get some bottles of water. I know it's hot. From here, we don't really need to use the tour guide.'

Whilst waiting outside, I spotted Ivan across the road chatting with Oliver and George. He looked emotional. I'd only seen him up to this point with a stern look on his face, so to see him looking stressed worried me.

With it being the first couple of days, I didn't really want to go over and ask, especially knowing he didn't speak English. I was worried that maybe we'd been spotted by locals who weren't happy with us filming there.

'He's just a little emotional right now.' George told us. While Ivan was gathering his thoughts across the road, Oliver strolled over to us.

'Ivan is a little upset, visiting this neighbourhood again has brought back some terrible moments in his life.' We continued walking still totally clueless as to why.

'I wonder what's happened with Ivan,' Troi whispered to me as we walked a little further. 'I never imagined him getting upset'.

'I'm not too sure, but it must be something bad if it's made him cry.'

The atmosphere felt a little strange. As we reached the height of the road, George whispered to us that Ivan was ex-Colombian Special Forces. 'He was involved in the conflict back in 2002, so I think he is a little upset to be back.' The group was stunned.

Suddenly out of nowhere, Ivan made a brave decision to tell his story on camera and they wanted Troi to do the interview. Troi was fine with it. With him being slightly younger than the rest of us, Chanel, Amber and myself were a little worried about how he would handle it, not least because we weren't totally aware of what had happened with Ivan.

The day suddenly turned from a light, touristy day to quite a deep one. Troi and Ivan got mic'd up ready for the interview and off they went.

Whilst we had a bit of down-time, I thought it would be a good idea to chat with some of the locals. I got speaking with one of the shop owners who told me how people in the neighbourhood used to a obey a curfew set by the gangs. She said most of the time people were afraid to leave their homes. It seemed that because I'd spoken with a local off-camera, I got more conversation out of them about real life in Medellín.

After chatting for a good twenty minutes, I walked back over to Chanel and Amber, who were sitting in the sun.

They looked worried.

Chapter Twenty

'What's up with you two?'

Chanel looked over to where Troi and Ivan were filming.
'Look at Troi - he looks upset too. I wonder what Ivan's
telling him?'

Nobody could guess. Obviously, we'd been told that he'd
been involved in the special forces and the conflict, but we
didn't know the full story. A couple of minutes later, I
noticed Ivan pull something from around his neck. It looked
like some sort of necklace. I said to the others; 'What's he just
passed to Troi?'

Suddenly Troi burst into tears. I wanted to run in. Even
though I'd only known him a few weeks, he felt like a little
brother, and to see him upset got to me.

'Guys, let's leave them to finish the interview and then we
can find out what's gone on.' George said.

Both Ivan and Troi turned to the road and pointed at the
centre.

'I think he's passed Troi his dog tag,' Amber said. 'You
know, the ID badge you get in the military.'

We all stood there for a good ten minutes waiting for the
interview to finish. I was desperate to find out what he'd
handed to him. After it ended, we all ran over to Troi to find
out exactly what had happened. While the girls were
hugging Troi, I heard Johnny say to Ivan; 'You're a brave
man. Thank you for sharing your story with us.'

It was becoming clear that something terrible had
happened in the past around the very place we were stood.
To see a grown man cry was enough, but to then see Troi
crying made me question exactly what had been said. Troi
was struggling to get his words out. With everyone stood
around him I think the whole scene and story had really got
to him.

Johnny stepped in, 'I think it's time we go for some food. There's a little restaurant across the road - is everyone OK with that?' I wasn't too concerned about the food at the time. I just wanted to know the story, but we agreed, and as we all made our way across the road to the restaurant, Troi mumbled 'Look at this - Ivan gave it to me'.

I looked down. It was a dog tag. Without asking, Troi broke down again.

'Ivan told me how he was involved in the conflict working for the Colombian military in this neighbourhood back in 2002. He told me many of his friends and colleagues died here. It was the first time he's returned.'

I couldn't believe what I'd just been told. 'Wow, mate that's some deep shit, no wonder your upset. So, how come he's given you the dog tag?'

Troi replied; 'It belonged to one of his friends who died here. He wanted to give it to me.'

As we walked into the restaurant, I said to Troi, 'I bet that was a difficult interview bro. We'll have a proper chat when we're back at the hotel if you want.'

The mood around the table was obviously a little low. The story had been totally unexpected. One minute we were joking around with tourists, then suddenly we were involved in this deep story. I suppose that was all part of filming a documentary. Things changed from one second to the next - it was what made it so exciting to be part of.

We eventually started back on our mission to climb to the top of the neighbourhood, and we had finally reached the electric stairs. It was crazy and almost looked like an outdoor shopping mall. We were told earlier in the day by the tour guide that they were built in 2011. It used to take the locals over 30 minutes to climb to their homes prior to them being built.

Seeing an escalator back home seems completely normal, but seeing it in Colombia felt slightly strange, especially with it being outside. As we approached the first set of stairs, we were greeted by a security guard. At first, I thought nothing of it, but by every single set of stairs stood security monitoring every move. Even though I felt completely safe, having guards there made the trip up the favela that little bit more intimidating.

What was a five-minute trip up the escalators, took over thirty minutes. Each time the four of us reached the top, the crew asked us to repeat the walk so they could catch it from several angles. At times I felt like a robot, but I knew that it would be an important shot. You get a sense of what looks good cinematically after a while when you're on television, and this was one of those moments. Well, more than one!

As I stepped off the escalators for the final time, I was shocked to see the amount of people wondering about. Most of them being tourist. George said we were free to have a look around. I wasn't too sure what there was to look at until I walked a little further. The place was full of food stalls and locals selling souvenirs.

As we walked through the busy streets of Comuna 13 the cameras were following our every move. Chanel spotted one of the stalls selling Pablo Escobar T-shirts. 'Ey, check that T-shirt out. I want it.'

She then walked over and pointed at the T-shirt; 'Excuse me, how much is that?'

The female t-shirt seller replied, '80,000'.

Chanel's eyebrows raised, 'Sorry, what?' With it only being the first couple of days in Colombia no one really understood the currency. After discussing with Oliver, we worked out that it was around £20.

She was keen to buy it. George saw it as a good opportunity to interview one of the locals, so agreed to buy it for her. He called over Chanel. I could hear them in the distance - 'Seeing as though she is selling Pablo T-shirts it might be a good opportunity to ask her a few questions about him?'

Chanel walked back over to the stall and handed the 80,000 pesos to her. At first the stall owner didn't seem too keen on chatting in front of the camera. After Chanel worked her magic, she was happy to chat. I was surprised she spoke English.

'Do you sell many of these T-shirts to tourists?' Asked Chanel.

'Yes, many people buy these T-shirts, not just tourists. It's one of our best sellers...I think it is the last one.'

I remember thinking that I wouldn't walk around wearing a Pablo Escobar t-shirt, but I could see why people would buy them as a souvenir or gift. Chanel went a little deeper into conversation.

'What do you think of Pablo Escobar? Was he a good or bad man?'

'He's a very sexy man.' She replied.

'He brought a lot of money to the area. People have mixed views on him.'

With the lady saying he brought a lot of money into the area I was keen to find out if she'd been given any money personally. I popped my head over Chanel.

'Did he give you any money?'

She replied, 'No he didn't give me any money, although I know of families who have been helped by him in the past.'

It was becoming clear that many of the locals didn't really want to speak about the so-called 'Drug Lord' Pablo Escobar. I wasn't sure if they were afraid to bad mouth him, or if they genuinely appreciated some of the things he had done.

The sun was setting, and it was coming to the end of the day. We'd been out in the heat for over five hours. After walking through the market stalls, we found a place to sit down and chill. What started out as a touristy chilled day was turning in to a long tiring one.

I took a seat on the curb and I looked over to Troi. He looked shattered! 'You OK, Troi mate?'

Suddenly, he went as pale as a ghost. He replied whilst short of breath, 'Not really mate, my chest is killing'. I couldn't work out if the 30c heat had taken its toll, or the stress of the interview with Ivan was playing on his mind. Either way, it was very worrying.

Amber shouted over to the crew, who were busy setting up a drone for the final shots.

'Guys, I don't think Troi is very well.'

Chapter Twenty-One

We were at the very top of the favela. The crew were worried that the altitude was playing a part in Troi's wellbeing. George made the decision to halt filming and I think the four of us were slightly relieved.

After several bottles of water and snacks, Troi felt well enough to set off back down the escalators. You could tell by the way he was walking that he still wasn't feeling great. With the cameraman and soundman at Troi's side, I had the job of carrying the equipment on their behalf.

As we reached the bottom of the stairs, Troi suddenly felt unwell again. The decision was made to rush him straight to hospital. As he and Oliver whizzed off in a backup car, we made our way back to the coach, which was parked up where it had dropped us.

After getting back on the coach, everyone was a lot quieter than normal. We were all concerned about Troi. I was worried that it was something more than sun stroke and he'd be told that he couldn't carry on with the journey.

I turned to Chanel and Amber who were sat opposite me. 'I hope he's OK'.

'I know,' Amber replied. 'He's had a hard day, especially after the whole Ivan story.'

'Hopefully they'll tell us a bit more about it when we get back,' added Chanel.

As we arrived back at the hotel, George received a text message from Oliver.

'Good news guys. Troi should be OK to continue. He's been told to rest for a day.'

There was a sigh of relief in the air. The last thing anyone wanted was someone being sent home for illness. After such a long day, we were all told that filming was done and we could get a rest ahead of what would be another early start, and a day where only three of us would be on-screen.

Two minutes later, I headed up to my room to sleep. Suddenly, there was a knock on my door. It was the girls. Chanel had a smirk on her face.

'Err, me and Amber have been having a chat in my room. Do you fancy going out?'

'What do you mean? Like 'out, out'?'

'Yeah, what else do you think we mean?' they said, laughing.

It took them precisely two minutes to talk me into it. Don't get me wrong, I was slightly worried. Not only did we have to be up early the following morning, but I had the worry of being on a night out in Colombia alone with two British girls. Surely it was going to be a bad idea!

A few minutes later the girls headed to their rooms to get ready. I felt slightly guilty knowing Troi was in bed still recovering whilst we were getting ready for a night out. I had to knock on his room to see if he wanted to join us.

'Troi – it's Louis, are you up mate?'

He answered the door.

'How are you feeling?'

'Not too good. The doctors just told me to rest, so hopefully I'll be OK in the morning.'

He didn't look great, so I didn't even bother asking him to join us on the night out. The answer was obviously going to be a no, so I left him to it.

Just as I was walking out of the room, I noticed the dog tags Ivan had given him on his bedside cabinet. I felt slightly sorry for him.

'If you need to chat about anything just knock on my door mate.' I then realised after I'd left the room that if he were to knock, I probably wouldn't be in.

As I made my way back through the corridor, I bumped into the cameraman.

'Night Lou, see you bright and early in the morning.'

I kind of felt bad, knowing I'd been told to stay in, but there was no time for guilt.

I was ready for my first night in Colombia, and I was doing my best to keep it under wraps. After ten deep breaths, I sneaked out of my room like James Bond and made my way to Chanel's room. Music was blasting from her speakers. She hadn't exactly made it discreet that we were going out. I was worried we were going to get a knock on the door from one of the crew telling us to keep it quiet and they might then spot that we were all dressed up ready for our night on the town.

I was totally unaware where we were heading. We'd been told earlier in the day that Medellín was a good night out. We just didn't know where to go.

After cleaning out the minibar it was time to leave. It was pitch black. This was the first time we'd left the hotel without a camera following us. As I stepped out the reception door, I felt a sense of relief. Obviously, they were keeping us in for our own safety, but after four tough days, the night out was needed.

With the little knowledge we'd been given on the first day by Oliver, we made our way to the square. Walking through the streets alone with two young women felt slightly unnerving. Up to this point, we'd had security following us at all times. Going out was a risk.

After a good ten-minute walk, we reached the square. It looked like a completely different place to the last time we seen it on the first day. It was lit up like a busy night out in Manchester. The place was packed. I looked to Amber and Chanel and smiled.

'Well, I wasn't expecting this!'

I think the three of us were shocked. I wasn't too sure what I was expecting, but it wasn't what I was looking at. As we made our way around the square looking for a place to have our first drink, we were approached by a young male. I panicked and said. 'Come on, let's keep walking'.

He replied; 'Guys, guys, where are you from?'.

Chanel started talking to him. Who the fuck is this guy? There was no way I was waiting around in the middle of the street chatting with some random Colombian guy. Two minutes later and we found ourselves in a bar. It turned out that he was one of the bar staff who hang around the streets trying to bring in customers. Magaluf tactics, I suppose.

The place was packed with tourist and locals. We'd only been in the bar five minutes before the three of us were up dancing to some random Colombian music. I was surprised that we hadn't been offered any cocaine. I expected to turn up at a bar and it was going to be as simple as, 'Would you like anything else with your drink?'

After two double vodkas we made our way to a nightclub. This time it was a little shadier. I got the feeling that the place we'd just entered was run by some sort of gang. The three of us were searched and ID's were checked.

As we approached the bar, I shouted to Chanel and Amber - 'Wait there, I'm just nipping to the toilet. Don't move!' I was bursting, but I was worried if I left them, I wouldn't find them until the following morning. It must have been a second after entering the toilet I got a tap on my shoulder.

'Ey!'... I looked over my shoulder to see some huge man stood there.

'Cociana?'

I suddenly stopped weeing. 'Err, no I'm good mate.'

I didn't know what to say. Why did I just call him mate? I was worried I'd offend him by saying no. I was there on a journey to find out about cocaine, not sniff it. There was no way I was going back to the hotel off my face.

I was shocked at his response - 'No problem.'

As I made my way out of the toilet he shouted, 'Have a good night brother'.

I thought, wait am I in Colombia here? Why is everyone being so friendly? I got slightly paranoid thinking he was just checking me out to see if I was a tourist and then he would jump on me later.

When I got back to the bar, Chanel and Amber had already got the shots in. The night was turning into a messy one! I felt like I was on holiday with all my mates. I was enjoying it that much I didn't even think about getting up early for filming.

It got to 4am and the square was still rocking! After a long day filming and hours partying, I was ready for bed and it seemed that I wasn't the only one. Even though we were absolutely steaming and loving the nightlife, we made the sensible decision to call it a night.

After stumbling out of the club, we set off walking back to the hotel. I'd been told by one of the locals to try and avoid taxis at that time of night. Apparently because we were tourists they'd try and charge a stupid fare. I felt safer walking anyway - it must have been the drink!

Just as we got out of Medellín Square, we were greeted by street dealers on pretty much every corner. They were offering us one gram of cocaine for 20,000 pesos. It worked out at around £5. Nearly ten times as cheap as back home. I wasn't interested. I just wanted to get back to the hotel. Chanel having tattoos and looking slightly Colombian was attracting loads of attention. It was the last thing I needed at 4am in the morning.

I looked to her - 'Chanel, hurry up!'. The dealers wouldn't leave us alone.

What should have been a ten-minute walk turned in to a good thirty-minute trip. I was also expecting to get back to the hotel to see Johnny standing there asking where we had been.

That wasn't the case, so I thought it would be a good idea to sit outside on the balcony and chat with Chanel whilst Amber made her way to bed. We must have been sitting there five minutes before I started to nod off. It was time for bed! Medellín had lived up to its name for the nightlife, and that was without the cocaine!

Chapter Twenty-Two

Two loud knocks at the door shook me from the first couple of hours of what my body had hoped would be a long and restful sleep.

'Louis, it's George. Can you answer the door please?' came the shout, a tone of repetition clearly present.

It was the last thing I wanted to hear in the morning after a messy night. I opened the door to a stern look on George's face.

'We're all waiting for you downstairs. We have to leave in less than one hour for filming. Can you hurry up please!'

I knew I was in a bit of trouble. I threw on a pair of shorts and ran downstairs. I remember thinking, there is no way Chanel and Amber are downstairs ready before me. We didn't even have time to discuss a plan of what to say if we were questioned as to why we'd been out. As I walked out of the door to take a seat for breakfast, all eyes were on me. I felt like a naughty school kid. I looked to be the last one down. George looked fuming.

'Good night last night?'

I was stuck for words. I looked to Chanel and Amber for help. They'd seemed to have already been told off because their heads were face down. 'Err...yeah it wasn't too bad, I'm feeling pretty fresh to be honest.' It was a complete lie. I felt like shit!

With the three of us going out I knew there wasn't much chance of us getting kicked off the show, but I still had a slight worry. As the breakfast turned up at the table George said, 'Can everyone listen up please?'

I swallowed something dry, probably my pride.

'We are aware that Chanel, Louis and Amber went out last night. You're all adults, so obviously we can't stop you from going out, but if you do again whilst we're we are in Medellín, please tell us.'

We'd been let off the hook. I felt slightly guilty. As much as I was there to make a great TV show, I felt the night out was needed. I looked over to Chanel and Amber who looked to have a smirk on their faces.

'What you's laughing at?'

I got no response. With the night flying by I'd completely forgotten that Troi was back at the hotel resting. There was still no sign of him at breakfast. I shouted out to the group 'How's Troi?'

George replied whilst laughing, 'Well you three clearly wouldn't know because you were too busy going out getting pissed.' After a short while everyone had a little giggle about us going out. If I'd have known it was going to be that easy, I think the three of us would have done it on the first night!

'Yeah, he's still not 100%. He will be resting again today so it's up to you three to hold the fort.'

Chanel responded; 'Argh, I hope he's OK. What is it we're doing today? Hopefully not much with this hangover!'

'If you can all quickly get ready and make your way back downstairs to reception. We will have a quick briefing for the day once you're back down.'

Each day that passed seemed to give us less time to prepare for the day. It didn't help that I was getting up thirty minutes before the call time. Leaving myself ten minutes for a shower and shave was pushing it. After running around my room like a fly, I was ready for another day filming and this time, I made sure I was the first one back down to reception.

Ten minutes passed and there will still no sign of Amber or Chanel. I was worried that they'd fallen back asleep. While I waited, my thoughts rewound to our night out in Medellín Square.

It felt like a mad experience. With the whole trip starting quietly, I was expecting things to get a lot more interesting.

Shortly afterwards, Amber and Chanel turned up at reception.

George began speaking. 'Ok, I think we're all here now. This morning we're going to be visiting Pablo Escobar's grave. The main objective is to chat with some of the people there. Maybe ask them why they're visiting etc... like yesterday at Comuna 13. We have been told it can be extremely hostile, so please listen to Oliver's instructions on the coach. There is more filming planned for the afternoon so drink plenty of water, it's going to be a long day.'

Chapter Twenty-Three

Visiting Pablo Escobar's grave wasn't something I wanted to do in all honesty. However, I knew it was coming, with it being such a huge part of Medellín culture and its tourist attractions. I felt slightly weird that I'd be visiting a grave of someone I didn't even know. Obviously, it was all part of the documentary, but I'd just never seen the fascination of visiting someone's grave just because they were famous.

After another forty-minute coach journey we'd nearly arrived at the cemetery. As we drove up the long narrow road, Oliver told us that there would most likely be gang members hanging around the cemetery. He also told us of the strict one-hour timeframe we had for the visit. It all seemed a little dodgy.

As I stepped off the coach in the main car park, I felt a strange aura in the air. I had a picture in my head before arriving of it being a huge field with one grave in the centre. It was the complete opposite. It looked like a normal British cemetery, but it certainly didn't feel like one.

I only had to turn my head slightly before seeing three men standing fifty metres away staring at us. I presumed they'd been made aware we were visiting. They looked different to anyone like I'd seen in Colombia. They were clearly part of some gang. It was the most nervous I'd been since arriving.

The men, muscly and with bald heads, were dressed smartly in loose short-sleeved shirts, all-white, but with navy coloured dark trousers. They seemed like lookouts for the area and it felt like as if there was any trouble, they'd be deciding how it ended.

Whilst the crew unloaded the equipment from the coach, I had a little time to chat with Oliver.

'Are they the people you told us about on the way here?'

'Yes, they are most likely active gang members. Sometimes the cemetery can be very dangerous, especially at night-time.'

It really did feel like a strange atmosphere. Oliver was the only person who had visited before. We followed him across the grass field towards the grave we were there to see. The most famous drug lord in history...Pablo Escobar.

As I approached the grave, I stopped and stood there a little surprised. It certainly wasn't what I was expecting. There was a small headstone with his name, date of birth and date of death on it. The whole thing looked quite worn and old.

For a man who was known for his wealth and power, I was expecting a lot more. Maybe something like you see in the films, where the tombstones are bigger than small houses. Without being disrespectful, I wouldn't have noticed it was Pablo Escobar's grave if I had been randomly walking past it.

Next to Escobar's headstone were six others. They looked to be close family and friends who had also died.

The cameras were rolling. Johnny asked me, 'What do you think of the grave then Louis. Is it what you expected?'

I froze. I was a little confused, I didn't know what to say. Visiting family members graves can be uncomfortable enough, never mind a man who was known for so much violence and death.

'To be honest I feel a little strange about it all. I can see why people who were close to him might visit, family and friends, but tourists? Is that the right thing to do?'

The conversation continued with Amber and Chanel joining in. I think the three of us were a little confused as to why we were there. It almost felt like 'OK, we've seen it now, let's go'. There are only so many times you can look at a small plaque.

Not long after, a bus full of tourists pulled up into the car park. There must have been a good twenty people getting off. I couldn't work out why so many people would want to visit, but I was close to finding out.

I think Johnny could see that the whole scene wasn't going great, so he called us over for a quick chat.

'Listen guys, I know it's hard and not the most interesting thing to cover but trust me, after this, things are going to get a lot better.'

A few minutes later and the grave was full of tourists. Most of them were taking photos and the odd few attended with flowers to pay their respects. I took a moment out to people-watch whilst they had a look around. It was interesting to watch every single one of them act slightly differently. Some of them were laughing, not directly at the grave, but not showing any emotion, while others were getting quite upset.

The longer I was there the more I wanted to leave. I knew we had to finish the scene. There was no way the crew was travelling to the other side of Medellín for a few shots of us standing still. We were there to speak with people.

Shortly after it got a little quieter, we finally had the chance to speak with some of the visitors. Surprisingly most of them was happy to be on camera. We spoke with a family who were visiting from the other side of Colombia. They'd travelled over three hours to visit the grave.

'He did good and bad,' they told me. 'We think he was a great man.'

I'd been in Medellín for four days and I hadn't heard one local say a bad word about Pablo Escobar. I wasn't sure if they were afraid to say anything negative or they genuinely were all for what he stood for.

It was time to leave the cemetery and head back to the hotel. I'd been in Colombia for four days and I was certainly learning a lot about Medellín and the country itself, just not a lot about cocaine - the real reason we were there.

Chapter Twenty-Four

Later in the day, after a short rest, it was time to head back downstairs to find out what the plan was for the evening. I was expecting big things after Johnny told us the trip was about to get a lot more interesting. Not that I wasn't enjoying it. I'd just had enough of the sight-seeing. I wanted to see the deeper side of Colombia.

'Hope you've had a good rest. Troi unfortunately isn't well enough to film again tonight. We're hoping he will be OK for the morning. The plan was for Troi and Chanel to head to the jungle tomorrow, but we may have to change things around depending on how Troi is feeling. We can't expect him to walk through the jungle with a bad chest.' Said Johnny.

I was a little gutted. I'd been told prior to arriving in Colombia that there was a possibility of going into the jungle, but it sounded like I wouldn't be going.

'So, what is it me and Amber are going to be doing?' I asked Johnny.

'Depending on Troi, you and Amber will be heading to the North of Colombia to a place called Turbo.'

I knew we'd be splitting sometime in the trip. I just wasn't expecting it to be so early. By this point we'd all formed a close bond, so I don't think any of us were keen on leaving each other.

'Before that, we need to focus on tonight. Chanel, with Troi still resting, you will be interviewing alone. You'll be visiting a trap house with me and half the crew. Louis and Amber, you will be with George, visiting a gentleman named Juan David in one of the more well-known areas for drugs and crime.'

I didn't know how to react. Juan David sounded intimidating enough, but to be then told the area we'd be visiting was well known for drugs and violence put the pressure right up. I thought we'd been let off compared to Chanel, but she was buzzing.

After saying our goodbyes to Chanel and wishing her the best of luck, Amber and I headed back outside to our vehicle. With the crew splitting up into pretty much two groups, the coach felt quite empty.

On the way, we were briefed on the schedule for the afternoon. We were told that we would meet Juan David at a community centre he ran. He'd then walk us around the neighbourhood telling us a bit about the area and its problems with cocaine. Obviously while this was happening, we would have the pleasure of interviewing him. I wasn't too sure what I was going to ask.

As the coach arrived, everyone was a little edgy. We were told by Oliver to stay in our seats whilst he went and met Juan David to get the all clear. As I looked out the window, I noticed that it seemed a very deprived area. Everywhere I looked there was an addict standing, staring at nothing. I saw so many random things. Horses carrying things for people up and down the street. Believe it or not we even saw a guy walking with a kitchen sink.

I was more worried about being stabbed with a needle than being kidnapped by a gang. A few minutes later Oliver jumped back on the coach.

'OK guys listen up. He's ready. Once we are in the building, you always listen and follow Juan David's instructions. He will tell you what is going to happen for the afternoon.'

As we stepped off the coach, we made our way single file across the road. We were the subject of stares from the entire town. The building we needed to get to was only 50 metres away, but it felt like 50 miles at that moment.

Oliver was the first one to make his way up the stairs. There were metal gates at the top with a buzzer to let people in. As we reached the top, we were greeted by a man who welcomed us in. I wasn't too sure if it was Juan David, but I wasn't asking. He told us to take a seat in one of the waiting rooms. The place reminded me slightly of a school.

As I nervously took a seat, I dared to say a word. The crew and Amber were silent, and you could hear each of us breathing. After ten minutes of awkward silence, a gentleman walked in and told us Juan David should be ready to speak to us shortly. I was incredibly anxious. My palms were sweating.

It was the first time Amber and I would be interviewing someone as a pair. I was a little concerned as to what type of questions I could ask, knowing it was a completely different interview to any previous ones. It was probably a bit late, but I asked George, who was directing, whether any topics would be off-limits with Juan David. Oliver gave us our answer.

'If he doesn't like the question, he simply will not answer.'

I still didn't have a clue what I was going to ask. I was hoping Amber would pull a few questions out of her sleeve. After patiently waiting for nearly an hour, Juan David walked in. He had a real presence. Very intimidating. His gait was long and slow, he had a ponytail down his back, and he was incredibly muscly. I didn't know whether to shake his hand, bow or cry. He was a beast! I chose the handshake and he nearly broke my hand in the process. When he spoke, the room echoed.

'Today I will take you around my neighbourhood. As you already know, it is known for gang violence, so it is important you stay with me at all times. If you stick by my side, you will be safe.'

I swallowed heavily. I was worried.

'Firstly, I will be taking you to a prostitute's house. You can interview her first. We will then visit an old lady who has an interesting story to tell. After this I will walk you around the neighbourhood to a street which is known for its drug addicts.'

I wasn't exactly sure why he was showing us around the prostitute's house, but there was no way I was questioning him. The crew knew that if we had any chance of good footage then we had to go with it.

Juan David then asked us to put on some T-shirts. He told us they we're to show the people in the neighbourhood we were part of his organisation.

'Remember to stay by my side at all times' he said. As we were all about to follow him out the door he suddenly stopped. 'There is a chance whilst walking around that we may be able to stop and speak with an active gang member. It all depends if he is happy to do the interview.'

My heart dropped. I wasn't sure what to make of it. I looked to the crew as if to say, 'Is that in the script?' It all sounded slightly sketchy, but it was exactly what I'd signed up for.

As we walked back down the stairs out on to the busy main street, you could feel the tension in the air. With the cameraman's eyes down the lens, George busy directing and the soundman listening in, all the pressure was on Amber and me to pull out a great interview.

It was a very similar set-up to the first day, meeting and interviewing Oscar. We would walk next to him and ask him a few questions, whilst he would point a few things out around the neighbourhood.

The interview started with a few light questions. Tell me a bit more about what you do in the area Juan? What does a normal day consist of in this neighbourhood? From the few people we'd interviewed up to then, we seemed to be getting very similar answers. 'There isn't much to do. It's hard for the children'. We got a completely different response with Juan. 'We have to deal with what we have. Here at the community centre we do our best to keep children and adults away from gangs and drugs whilst educating them.'

The interview was going so well that I'd overlooked the fact that we were in such a dangerous area. After walking a little further down the main street, Juan David suddenly stopped on the pavement. 'Ok we are here. There is a lady in here I would like you to meet.'

The house certainly didn't look like a place I wanted to enter. I couldn't work out if it was the prostitutes house or the home of some random gangster. Juan walked over to the door and started banging on it.

Two minutes later a woman popped her head out of the door. She looked confused! I wasn't sure she was used to a camera crew turning up at her home.

After a few seconds speaking with Juan, she invited us into the house. I didn't have a clue why, but me being polite said, 'Thank you for letting us in to speak with you'. I just had to go with it.

As I followed Juan David up the steep narrow stairs towards what looked like a flat, I couldn't get over the awful smell. The place reeked of urine and damp. I was in complete shock that someone could live with such a smell.

After climbing three flights of stairs, we reached the top of the building. As I walked through the door, I instantly noticed how small the place was. It was tiny! I could see the whole flat from the front door. There was a kitchen, one small bedroom and a main room.

I still didn't have a clue why we were there.
I noticed Juan speaking with the lady who had answered the door. Already I could see she looked quite upset. He turned to Amber and me.

'This lady would like to tell you a little story. This is the reason I have brought you here.'

The interview was supposed to be based around Juan David and the drug problems in the area, but we found ourselves chatting with one of the locals about her personal problems. With it being the start of the day, I wasn't too sure if Juan was testing us, or the lady who he had brought us to see genuinely had something of interest to tell us.

As the crew set up the scene, I noticed an elderly lady resting on a bed in the back room. I had a feeling she was going to be a prostitute. It was my worst nightmare. She looked ill and must have been eighty plus years of age.

Suddenly, the interview started. I say interview, but at first, it was more the lady telling us her story and us listening. It was the complete opposite to what I thought she was going to tell us.

'I used to work for the government as an advisor'.
I wasn't quite sure what kind, but she told us that she could no longer leave her home.

'Every time I go to sleep, I worry about not waking up again.'

I was guessing she'd been found out by a local gang? I had little time to take it in and I was a little confused. The interview was going so fast!

She then went on to tell us that her son had gone missing. He'd been missing for over two years, but apparently she was too afraid to go out looking for him. Both Amber and I were a little saddened. It was heart-breaking, but the interview couldn't become too personal. We cared about her, but we had to draw out her experiences as to how they were indicative of the area as a whole.

'What is life like, living around here?... is there lots of violence?'

'Yes, there is plenty of violence. I often hear gunfire on the street.'

I couldn't believe what I'd just heard. It was at that point I knew I'd underestimated the place we were in. She then went on to tell us how the gangs come around to her home each week to collect rent. The woman was already getting upset and Amber was in tears too.

Amber asked her what she thought would happen if she didn't pay the so called 'Rent'.

'I will be homeless. They will throw me out. The only way I make money is off what people give me.'

It was a really sad story - the worst we'd heard since arriving. It was becoming a very emotional day and I didn't have a clue where we'd be heading next. Juan David seemed to be very calm and collected about the whole situation, as if he'd done it all before.

As we were about to walk out of the door downstairs to say our goodbyes, the woman told us she had cancer. It was a huge statement! I suddenly broke down. I felt so sorry for her. After everything she'd already been through losing her son and finally being displaced, she had been told she had cancer. She said she didn't want to say it on camera because she didn't want the sympathy. I gave her the biggest hug.

I asked her why she isn't in hospital trying to get help.

'I can't afford to go. Plus, if I do leave my home, I will be killed.'

She was in real pain and I felt terrible that I couldn't help.

Chapter Twenty-Five

After saying our goodbyes, we set off walking back down the street. It was obvious, looking at the people in the area, that they had a lot of respect for Juan. Despite that, I still worried that anything could go off at any time. With an hour of our time having been used to talk with the lady at her home, we were keen to get to know in detail about the effect that cocaine was having on the area more broadly.

With the main street heaving with noise and activity, the soundman thought it would be sensible to go off the beaten track and move to the quieter, side streets. I wasn't too sure at the time, but Juan seemed to be OK with it, albeit making it very clear that there were boundaries in the area, and they weren't to be crossed.

Even as we moved only a short distance, the streets started to change. There seemed to be less people wandering about, but lots of people watching from a distance, from houses and street corners. I opened with a question to Juan; 'How is cocaine affecting this area in particular?'

The response was quite shocking. 'Massively. There is a street I will be taking you to soon which is known as the drug addict street. We do our best to try and keep the addicts in the same area to avoid the children seeing and getting involved.'

'OK, so you have one street where addicts live, if they are from this area?'

'Correct.'

I didn't quite know what to make of it. I'd heard and seen back home of addicts living out of one house and sharing, but a whole street?

'As we walk around the area now, I feel quite safe. What would happen to me if I was to walk here alone?'

He giggled. 'You would probably get ten metres down the road before the whole area knows you are here. There are people watching everywhere. They would inform the relevant people and you would be taken off the street almost immediately.' I laughed nervously.

There seemed to be something that Juan was holding back. I just couldn't work out what it was. With the sun setting fast, we had around an hour before we had to leave the neighbourhood. We were told earlier in the day that staying past dark was a complete no-no.

Suddenly, we'd reached the very street Juan was talking about, the 'Addicts Street'. The atmosphere changed rapidly. Juan put his arms across Amber's and my stomach to stop us going any further.

'Ok, we are now entering the street I mentioned earlier. I can tell you there will be people injecting on the street and some of the things you may see could be shocking. The users may also react badly to our presence, but they have been informed we are visiting. As you probably know, drug users can be incredibly volatile and unpredictable so keep your eyes peeled.'

I was nervous to say the least. Obviously, you see people in the centre of Manchester and London off their faces on all sorts of drugs, but this felt different. As we started to walk down the street we continued with our questions.

'So, Juan, can you explain a bit more about this street you have brought us to?'

'As you look around the street you can see the drug paraphernalia everywhere. Most people around here are addicted to cocaine.'

'How can they afford to pay for it?' Amber asked.

'Good question. 90% of the people around here smoke 'basuco'. This is basically the rubbish left over from the coca paste. People can buy this on the streets much more cheaply than cocaine, usually around $1 per gram.'

I was keen to know more about basuco, but I thought it would be best to ask Juan after we left the street on which they were taking it. It must have only been thirty seconds before I spotted the first user. She was an elderly lady without any shoes on. She sat casually on the pavement injecting something. I couldn't believe what I was seeing.

'Do the police know about this street, Juan?'

'Of course, they see it the same as us. If the users are kept in one particular street, then it will hopefully avoid young children witnessing what you are seeing right now.'

I got the vibe that the police wouldn't dare enter. As we walked a little further down, the tension was building. I could tell that even Juan was nervous. More and more people started to gather on the street. It was almost a free for all. Everyone seemed to be just standing outside their homes, staring at us like zombies as we walked past. I felt a sense of sympathy for them. Not because they were drug addicts, but it was becoming obvious that the people around the area didn't really have any opportunities to gain an education or career. It was as if they'd just been put onto a street and left with no help.

As we came to the end of the street, I noticed a small shop on the corner. People stood outside smoking and injecting cocaine. There were needles all over the place whilst people were walking barefoot. It felt like something out of a horror movie.

I noticed a few of the locals outside the shop staring at us. Juan David said, 'We need to leave.'

When we turned off the street there was a sense of relief. I looked over my shoulder and stood there for a second taking everything in. Walking through that area almost felt like I was holding my breath underwater until reaching the other side and being able to breathe again. George wanted to go back through the street and film some of the shots from a different angle. Juan David told him it wasn't possible. It was too risky.

There wasn't much time left with Juan. As we headed back to the community centre, I still felt slightly confused about the whole basuco thing. I decided to ask him.

'So, you mentioned basuco. What exactly is it and what does it do?'

Juan replied, 'Basuco is mostly smoked, like a cigarette or sometimes with a self-made pipe. Even though it is known as rubbish, it is incredibly strong. Therefore, people get addicted to it.'

After several questions, I got to the bottom of basuco's real definition. It is a residual paste left at the bottom of the barrel after the pure cocaine has been produced. I felt I'd learned a lot during our time with Juan. In the UK taking cocaine is seen as an almost sociable drug, whereas Colombia seemed to be the complete opposite.

The night was closing in rapidly. Juan told us we could walk the long way around the neighbourhood back to the community centre. I didn't know how I felt about it at the time, but the rest of the team and I were desperate to get the interview with the gang member.

As we passed each house, the locals seemed to greet Juan individually. Very similar to when we met Oscar. Although we'd been in the neighbourhood around two hours, I hadn't seen one policeman. For an area known for drugs and violence, it felt as if they were purposely avoiding it.

After ten minutes walking, we'd reached a crossroads. Juan spoke up - 'Please stay by my side at all times around here. Do not cross the road.'

On the corner of every street stood what looked like active gang members. Young looking, baseball caps on, tattoos, just what you'd expect a Colombian gangster to look like. A few of them were on motorbikes, while others were on foot. I wasn't sure what was going on.

Juan David said; 'Wait on this corner! Do not move. I will be back in two minutes.'

Then suddenly he jogged off over the road into one of the houses leaving Amber, George, the soundman, cameraman and me standing alone on a street corner in the middle of one of the most dangerous places in Medellín. I started to panic.

'What's going on? Why has he left us here?'

Everyone seemed to remain calm except me. My first thought in my head was, 'They're going to take all the camera equipment and then kidnap us.'

With the soundman and cameraman being extremely experienced in hostile situations having worked in similar scenarios, they assured me everything was going to be fine.

'He's probably gone to talk with the bad boys to see if we can get an interview.'

The crew were stood there with £80,000 worth of equipment, quite relaxed. As if by coincidence, I noticed a police motorbike drive past. They stopped at the top of the crossroads. I heard one of the people on the corner whistle at the cops as if to say, 'Everything's fine here'. The police knew fully what was going on, yet they didn't seem to pay any attention to us being there.

Suddenly Juan came running back over - 'Sorry about that. Unfortunately, the gang member isn't willing to do an interview. If you come back next week that may change.'

I looked to George as if to say, 'No chance am I coming back here'. I'd just been standing in the middle of a ghetto under the impression we were in the shit, only to be told we had to come back another time.

After the panic, we'd finally arrived back at the community centre. Our time with Juan David was up. It was certainly an eye-opener. Seeing someone inject drugs knowing that there was nothing I could do to help them made me feel slightly guilty and the people we'd met, including the old lady, had all blown me away with the variety of their struggles.

It was time to leave and say our goodbyes to Juan. There was something about him that I couldn't quite work out. I didn't quite understand his role in the community. Was he well respected because he was an ex-gang member? Or was it simply because he's doing his best to help the locals in the favela?

'Thank you, Juan, for showing us around your neighbourhood. You've been great.' I said.

'No problem. If you do wish to come back next week, I'm sure we can arrange something.'

Everyone wanted to get back to the hotel safely and rest. But as we left the community centre and headed back to the coach, I spotted the lady we'd spoken to earlier in the day laughing on the street with her friend. She started waving at us.

'Adios'.

My heart sunk. Knowing she was stuck there with her son missing and then telling us she had cancer made me quite emotional. I then realised she'd told us she couldn't leave her home because she had fears of being killed, yet here she was outside relaxing and laughing. I wasn't sure what to believe.

As I jumped on the coach. The crew seemed to be happy with how the afternoon had gone, aside from being a little pissed off that we didn't get the gang member interview, but I knew there was still plenty to come. On route back, none of us could quite believe what we'd seen. The street we'd walked down with the addicts was something like I'd never seen before. The drive back to the hotel seemed long and I processed the day's events with goose bumps prickling my arms.

When we arrived back at the hotel, I noticed Troi in the distance on the reception balcony. He was finally up and out of his bed! I walked over to him and gave him a friendly hug.

'How are you feeling mate?'

'Much better now. I just can't wait to get started again.'

'Good man. So, you're all good for filming tomorrow then?'

'Yeah, I feel good to go.' said Troi. 'Anyway, how was today?'

'Mad! Some of the shit we saw today, you're probably fortunate you didn't come. Is Chanel back from the trap house yet?'

'No,' Troi replied. 'I've been sat here for the past couple of hours and I haven't seen them arrive back yet.'

I felt a little sorry for him. Obviously, the last thing anyone wanted was for one of the four presenters to fall ill whilst filming, but I could tell in his voice he was ready to go again.

It was time to head up to bed and get some well-earned rest. As I jogged up the stairs George shouted, 'Good work today Louis. I will issue a WhatsApp message shortly for the plans for tomorrow. Again, it's going to be a long one, so try to get an early night.'

I was so tired I don't even think I responded. I slammed my key in the door, flung it open and jumped on my bed! I hadn't sat down properly for over sixteen hours. My back and feet were killing me. Filming in Colombia was turning out to be a lot more difficult than I had expected. It wasn't just the physical side, but also the mental side.

Just as I was about to nod off, I received a message from George.

'Tomorrow morning, we will be splitting into two teams. Amber and Louis, you'll be heading to the North of Colombia. Chanel and Troi, you will be visiting the South. I will explain in detail tomorrow but please be checked out of your rooms by 5.00am.'

I was buzzing to see other parts of Colombia but there was also a doubt in my head about splitting into pairs. I didn't have a clue what we'd be doing there, but I was a night's sleep away from finding out.

When I woke, I felt like the sixteen-hour days were starting to take their toll. With the previous day being such a hectic one, I was hoping for a calm relaxed morning. I was leaving Medellín, however, and I would be travelling to the North of Colombia. I had around twenty minutes to pack, get myself ready and check out of the room.

With five minutes to spare I was down at reception ready for the day. I'd still not heard from or seen Chanel since she left for the trap house interview the night before. I was a little worried as there was no sign of her in her room nor at reception...

A few minutes later she appeared at the breakfast table with Troi and Amber.

'Chanel, you're alive! How was yesterday at the trap house?'

'Err, not great. He didn't turn up.'

Chanel told me how the person she was due to meet ran off after seeing police around the area. Ivan told her it was extremely rare to see police around that neighbourhood, so the interview was called off. It was becoming clear that we couldn't really rely on any of the criminals turning up. I suppose it just depended on how they were feeling on the day.

Amber explained what we'd been up to, meeting Juan David and the street drug addicts. They looked completely shocked. Despite the early wake-up call, everyone seemed to be in a good mood. We'd only been in Colombia five days, but it felt like I'd known the others forever. It was our final breakfast in Medellín as a group and I was sad. As much as I wanted to stay together as a four, I knew splitting up would be the only way to cover as much of Colombia as possible.

Shortly after, Johnny gathered everyone around the table for a morning briefing.

'As you know, today we will be splitting in to two teams. Troi and Chanel, you will be flying to the South visiting the jungle.'

Chanel jumped out of her chair; 'Sickkkk!'

'Louis and Amber, you will be heading to the North... by coach.'

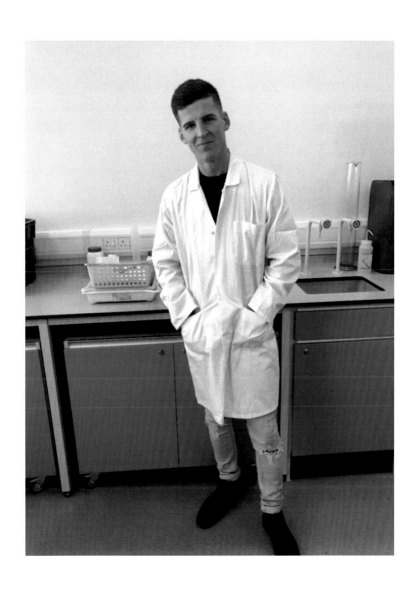

At the London University, about to get test results for cocaine samples

Amber, Chanel, the author and Troy - Ready for their first night out in Medellin

Visiting a Colombian town mural

Amber, Chanel, the author and Troy
On the Pablo Escobar Tour

With the children at the Favela Community Centre

Meeting the children at the Favela community centre

Outside electric stairs in one of the favelas

The author on the edge of one of Medellin's most dangerous ghettos

Waiting to board the helicopter

About to take-off for a Colombian military camp

The author with Colombian Major-General Jorge Vargas

The Author and Amber on a mission with the Colombian Military

About to accompany the military on a mission

En route back to the hotel after an eventful day

At the Colombian police anti-narcotics centre

With the Colombian Navy - about to go on a mission

Helping the crew film, while out with the Navy

Military lunch for the visitors

About to board the 'so-called' speedboat

On the way to a secret Trap House encounter in London

Chapter Twenty-Seven

After having all the necessary injections for the jungle, I thought I would be the one to go, but that wasn't the case and I was a little annoyed. It appeared as though Amber and I had drawn the short straw. Not only was I missing out on the jungle, I was heading to the other side of the country. On a coach!

Johnny continued whilst giggling. 'It should only take around eight hours. Don't worry, we will stop on the way. The views are beautiful.'

At that time of the morning, I didn't give two shits about the views. The only positive was the sleep I would get on the way. When Johnny had broken the news that we'd be going to the North and Troi and Chanel were heading into the jungle, I was disappointed. But that feeling soon faded with the clouds at sunrise, and before too long, I was buzzing to experience a new part of Colombia. Though we had no clue why we'd be heading to the North, that was what made the trip so exhilarating. I've always had an appetite for the unknown - I think it's where our human qualities truly come out and we show who we really are deep down.

Chanel and Troi had an idea of what was to come as the jungle was where the coca plant lived. But another reason surfaced for them going into the jungle together. Troi had the problem with his chest, and the jungle would require him to have a lot of energy. I don't think Amber would have held it together with Troi, whereas Chanel was a naturally upbeat person, fast becoming Troi's big sister on the trip. While Troi wasn't shy, Chanel brought the best out of him. From a production side of things, I believe they thought Amber and I might have been a bit more serious.

With breakfast over, it was time to say goodbye to Chanel, Troi and the rest of the team. There was a little confusion at first as to whether we would see each other again in Colombia. To our relief, George confirmed we would be meeting back up in Medellín later in the trip.

It was time for Amber and I to leave the hotel and head North. With the four presenters splitting into two, the crew also had to split. Oliver the fixer, Johnny the director and a cameraman were joining Amber and I, while George was heading to the South with Ivan, Chanel and Troi.

Before leaving, I'd been told that we were heading to a small city just outside of Turbo by the name of Apartadó. The minute we set off, I Googled it. After reading that there was a huge dock close to the location, I had a feeling we'd be meeting up with someone who exports cocaine by boat.

One hour into the drive Amber nudged me;

'Lou, we're stopping off here for a quick toilet break.'

As the sun blazed into my eyes, I sat up in my seat to find we were in the middle of nowhere. I was in a daze. I didn't have a clue where we were. We were surrounded by mountains. The only thing in sight was the petrol station we'd just stopped at. I'd said that I wasn't interested in the views, but that quickly changed. I'd never seen anything like it. The road had turned and twisted through the mountains for hours, and at times it felt like we were driving along the edge of a cliff.

Even though we weren't, it felt like we *were* in the jungle, with rain throughout most of the journey. The area had a weird aura. Mist circled the mountains as if it were a forcefield, and there was nobody about, apart from the odd farmer every couple of miles with a machete in his hand. We feared being stopped at any time and had also been advised that far right military randomly stop people in the road demanding money or their vehicle. Even when we stopped at cafes, people eyed us suspiciously and it was clear that we were outsiders in a sparsely populated area of the world.

Johnny noticed me staring.

'I told you the views were good.'

As I stepped off the coach to use the toilet I was greeted by several random chickens. There must have been twenty of them clucking around my feet. They looked angry. They were blocking my path to the toilet. I heard the crew laughing in the background. I didn't know whether to approach them or just back off. After an intense standoff, I managed to dodge around them, use the toilet and make my way back onto the coach. They were the first animals I'd come in to contact with since arriving in Colombia, and I'd just nodded off, so I didn't know how to react.

Knowing I was going to get stick the whole way to the North, I quickly turned the subject back to serious matters.

'So, Johnny, What's the plan once we arrive in Apartadó?'

'I think you'll be quite surprised by the person we're meeting. I'm going to be quite honest with you. You might panic but try not to. Tonight, you're going to be meeting with a cartel hitman.'

I looked at Amber in shock! We jumped out of our seats. What would he look like? How would it look on TV? Questions started to flood my mind. Within two seconds of finding out I started to get goose bumps. I knew we'd be meeting up with dangerous people, but I'd had no clue we were on our way to interview a hitman.

'Guys, I know this interview is going to be difficult, but try not to panic. You will be fine.'

My heart sunk. I remember thinking 'What on Earth is a young lad from Manchester going to ask a fucking hitman?'

It seemed crazy that I, with no experience presenting or interviewing, was about to get the opportunity to interview an active killer. As we continued to drive through the mountains, I just couldn't take my mind off the news I'd just been told. Usually when I'm travelling to somewhere new, I think about what the place looks like, what the locals might be like, but I couldn't stop thinking about the hitman.

With the coach going evidently quieter I started to think of some questions I'd like to ask. I started to jot them down on my phone. I think the first one I wrote down was the obvious one - 'How many people have you killed?'

I then found myself typing and typing until I had around thirty questions. I knew I was never going to get the time to ask all of them, so I narrowed them down to around ten. I still had no idea where we'd be meeting him, what he'd look like or anything else. It was the most nervous I'd been since arriving.

After a couple of hours, we stopped again, but this time it was at a small town in the middle of nowhere. There was one shop, a tiny hotel and about twenty fruit stalls. It looked like a neighbourhood in the Wild West. Not much going on, people walking about with holsters attached to there thighs, horse-drawn vehicles pulled over at the side of the road next to wooden stalls.

As the coach pulled up at the side of the road, I stepped off to try and find a toilet. Obviously, I'd never visited there before so I had no idea if it was dangerous. For all I knew it could have been run by the cartels.

As I walked towards the small supermarket, I was greeted by some of the locals. They seemed quite chilled out by our arrival. I couldn't get over the number of pop-up stalls selling fruit. It seemed to be the only thing from which anyone was making any money, apart from the drugs trade of course.

After paying a supermarket to use the toilet, I returned to the coach to find the driver and the rest of the crew standing outside scratching their heads. At first, I thought everyone was getting some fresh air, but I then realised the bonnet of the coach was open. We'd broken down.

Selfishly, the first thing that came into my head was the hitman. Knowing the interview was planned for later that evening, I knew any significant delay would surely mean it was off. But as nervous as I was, I just wanted to get it over and done with. Returning back later in the trip wasn't on my list of things to do and I had the feeling I wasn't the only one thinking that.

All eyes were on the driver. He seemed to be on the phone to someone shouting in Spanish. I would have loved to have known what he was saying, but he didn't sound happy.

The crew stood at the side of the coach discussing their next move, so I thought it would be a good time to ring home. The second my Mum answered all I heard was...

'Lou!!!'

It was Amber. I quickly ended the call and jogged back towards the coach.

'I think they're going to try pushing it.'

With the coach weighing over two tonnes, and that was without the luggage it was carrying, I knew we had no chance of pushing it alone. Luckily, the locals noticed we were struggling so they came over and helped. There seemed to be a real good sense of community. After thirty minutes pushing in the intense heat, the driver finally managed to start the engine. We got lucky.

After thanking the locals, we were back on the road again. Knowing I'd left my mum on a cliff hanger, I had to call her back. It was the first time I'd spoken to her in a few days, so she was totally unaware what I'd been up to. I wasn't quite sure how she'd react to me telling her I was on my way to meet a hitman.

Chapter Twenty-Eight

'What happened then? I was worried.'

'We broke down! I had to push the coach.'

She started laughing. Telling her about the interview we had planned would surely change that.

'Tonight, should be interesting. They've just told me I'll be interviewing a hitman!'

'Ask him how many people he has killed.'

I was baffled. My Mum seemed more excited than me at the time. Although I was quite blasé, I came off the call realising that I hadn't taken in the seriousness of the situation. You don't choose to get close to a killer! As a kid, I'd heard about Terry Waite, but I'd also remembered dozens of foreigners who had successfully visited other countries to investigate hitmen. Journalists have been captured, taken hostage, and even killed before. I didn't fancy joining that list.

Johnny had been all over the world making documentaries. We had the more experienced team with us in the North, and I had the feeling that we'd need it. That experience of having been in danger before and come out the other side was something Johnny had, and as much as we were a little anxious about the events to come, we knew we had the right man in our corner who would see us safe.

With the coach up and running again, at least for the time being, we struggled on. After nearly ten hours on the road we were less than five minutes away from Apartadó. As we approached the town, I was shocked by the large number of bars and restaurants. There was even a shopping mall. I'd only been there less than five minutes and it was already obvious that the area had a lot more income than just the drugs trade. There were a huge number of banana fields on the fringes of the route approaching Apartadó, and the town's route to money became clear. Without exaggerating there must have been millions of banana trees. I'd never seen anything like it!

We'd finally arrived at the hotel. After a long ten-hour journey, I couldn't wait to get off the coach, check-in and get a shower. I wasn't sure if we were in the right place. It looked like some sort of business park. I was shocked to see such a modern hotel in an area known for its violence and crime. It was the complete opposite of what I'd imagined. Luckily the hotel had a restaurant, so there was no need to leave. After checking in, Amber and I sat down to order food whilst Johnny came over to brief us.

'Tonight, we will be meeting up with a hitman. Unfortunately, we can't rely on criminals so there is a possibility that the interview will be called off. If Oliver does get the go-ahead, then we will make our way to the location, conduct the interview and then make our way back to our hotel. If all goes to plan, then we'll hopefully be leaving around 7pm.'

What if all didn't go to plan? I had a terrible thought in my head that Johnny was going to tell us we'd be meeting up in the banana fields hoping that the hitman didn't split. I was a little confused. Where exactly do you meet a hitman?

'Oliver will find out more information later, but for the time being try and think of some questions you may want to ask. Remember, the trip is based around discovering the effects cocaine has on people, so try to link your questions back to drugs.'

Again, it all seemed very blasé. Maybe it was just because I wasn't used to it. Most of the crew had been in those types of situations before but, for Amber and I, it was a totally new experience. Thinking of questions wouldn't be a problem. The issue would be remembering them and confidently asking them at the time of the interview. My head was spinning with random odd questions. Will we be sitting down interviewing him? Will he be alone? Johnny noticed me getting slightly anxious. Knowing he'd done several crime documentaries in the past, he gave me that bit of reassurance I needed.

'The best thing to do in these types of situations is to treat it like any other interview.' He told me. 'Remain calm and professional and you will be fine.'

Johnny stopped me on the way up to my room. He asked me to film a quick video on my phone once I'd settled in, a video diary. As I walked through the door I was shocked by the size of the room. It was huge. Once again, I had no idea how long I'd be staying in the hotel, so I opted to live out of my suitcase.

With less than two hours to go until the interview, I found myself pacing up and down the room. All sorts of questions were going through my head, but not ones I'd be posing to the hitman on camera. Will he be carrying a gun? What happens if he kicks off? What if one of his rival gang members sees him?

I knew it was the right time to hit the record button on my camera. I suddenly found myself rambling on for over ten minutes. After looking back at the video, I was just talking absolute nonsense. I could see in my own face I was nervous, so I tried re-recording.

By the time I'd recorded my video diary and showered, it was time to get ready. Picking an outfit to wear was near impossible. I still didn't know if the interview was going ahead but I knew I had to be on standby. As the clock ticked by, my room seemed to be getting noticeably hotter. I'm not sure if the nerves were kicking in, but the air conditioning had to be switched on full power.

I'd been told earlier in the day that Amber and I could ask any questions we wanted. Like the Juan David interview, our subject would simply refuse any question he didn't want to answer. With the little experience I'd gathered in the first few days of Colombia, I was feeling slightly confident. I was just worried I'd ask the wrong question and the situation might take a turn for the worse.

Seconds later, my phone buzzed, bang on 7pm. I grabbed it off the side. It was the go-ahead.

'Amber, Louis. Please meet down at reception ASAP!'

I ran to the bathroom, splashed my face and left the room. There was no way I was turning up late. I bumped into Amber on the way down. She looked as nervous as me. I think the both of us wanted to get it done and get back to the hotel safely.

As I took a seat next to Amber at the hotel bar, Oliver walked over.

'Hopefully we will be leaving soon. Remember to remain calm. If you are asked a question, try and answer to the best of your ability.'

While we sat at the hotel bar waiting, I shifted in my seat. I thought it would be a good idea to go over some of the questions I'd written down earlier in the day, but I knew no matter how many times I repeated them that nothing could prepare me for the hours ahead.

I wanted to try a new interview approach. I'd seen presenters on TV in the past question hitmen and they all seemed to ask the same thing: 'How much do you get paid?' I was intrigued to know that, but I felt it was necessary to make the interview unique. I tried thinking of questions the public would be interested in finding out, something that would spark some sort of reaction. I just had to be careful I didn't put myself, or anyone else in danger.

Amber went through her list of questions. Some of them were similar, a lot of them very interesting. Interviewing in a duo seemed to be a lot harder than alone or as a group. We decided it would be a good decision to take turns when asking questions.

The reception area was getting busier. I looked over my shoulder and noticed Oliver on the phone. I kept thinking that the interview would be called off and his facial expressions weren't looking too good.

Was it on or off?

Chapter Twenty-Nine

I swivelled my chair back towards the bar in disappointment. But then, quite suddenly, I heard Oliver shout to the pair of us.

'Ok, we need to go now! Is everyone ready to leave?'

I whispered to myself, 'This is it!'

As we made our way out to the hotel car park, there was a look of panic on everyone's faces. I was told to jump in Oliver's car with Amber and Johnny, while security and the rest of the crew would follow in a vehicle behind.

We set off in convoy along the dark road. It was dusty and a metre from the pavement, you would have had no idea what was going on. During the day, the roads would be packed out with people. Bananas fringed the fields, and with the fruit stalls, all we'd see is colour from sunrise to sunset. But at night, everything was pitch black. What was a pleasant sight by day, was dark and foreboding at night and even though we were moving, we felt boxed in.

Still unaware of the location, I started to fear the unknown. Oliver's phone rang. He must have only been on the call thirty seconds before it went dead. The car went silent. He turned his head towards me.

'Louis, please move to the middle seat to allow our man into the car.'

I didn't think anything of it until a few seconds later. 'Our man?' The penny dropped! Our man was the hitman.

'Wait, we're picking him up? The hitman is getting in the car?'

'Yes. We are only a few minutes away now so do it now while you can.'

It was the first time I'd seen Oliver stressed. The way he spoke and acted was different to usual. I suddenly felt very vulnerable. Not only was I about to interview a hitman but I'd just been told he was about to sit in the car next to me. It seemed very dodgy. I had to put all my trust in Oliver. Reality took a holiday as the surreal nature of our journey to Colombia flooded into the car. It was as if nobody dared to breathe.

As we continued to drive along the seemingly never-ending road, I started picturing the worst. What if we were kidnapped? You read about those sorts of things happening all the time. Having no control over the situation was making it a lot harder than I had first imagined. The adrenaline was pumping, and I knew that if we were to pull off the interview safely and effectively then I needed to remain calm.

At school, I was never afraid to speak out, no matter who I was talking to. But as I matured, I realised that I needed to be a bit more sensible in what I was saying. I tried to build up an aura around me, but I got nervous about slipping up. Eventually, during secondary school, I came out of myself, becoming a confident person. I still get nervous at times but getting over that initial feeling and doing something that you can look back on with pride is everything.

My Mum, who has a public-facing job, has previously talked about wanting to snap at a customer, but she's always said, that for the sake of a couple of seconds, to breathe then think of what you're saying. I didn't do that previously, but it's become a way of conquering that feeling of being terrified by what can feel like a 'locked door' situation. Smashing through that door time and time again has become part of who I am, and never would that be more important than in the next few hours.

After switching seats, I found myself staring out of the car window looking for the hitman. Probably not the best idea. Suddenly the car stopped! I couldn't see anybody.

Oliver whispered: 'This is where we will be picking him up. He shouldn't be long.'

Suddenly, I heard a loud bang that sounded as if it had come from near the window on my right. No one said a word. No one breathed. Even the air around us seemed to stop moving and, in the dank stillness of the car, I was hyper-aware that anything could happen. It was pitch-black apart from tiny pools of light that sat below a few carelessly placed streetlights.

The door handles suddenly popped. Two men, no older than twenty-five stood there.

The car following us suddenly pulled up. The painfully bright headlights reflecting off the wing mirror made sight impossible. Oliver took off his seat belt and got out of the car. I could hear them chatting in Spanish, but I couldn't see them. I couldn't believe the situation I was in! I looked to Amber and laughed sarcastically.

Seconds later, the lights of the car behind were turned off. I noticed the two men getting slightly agitated as they stood in the street. I had expected them to have some sort of mask or balaclava, but that wasn't the case.

Minutes later the door to my right popped open. In jumped the hitman. When you see a hitman on TV, they're always grown up, aren't they? Aged a little, worn in and worn out, at least thirty-five to forty. But this guy was young and fragile. He was quite edgy and shaky. He had a kind of strange vibe about him.

I didn't have a clue what to say to him. How do you greet a hitman? I nodded and said 'Ola.' I got no response but a look of intensity.

The car we were in suddenly felt like it had been squashed! With Amber sat to the left of me and the hitman to the right I had no room for movement and there was no way I was leaning on him. Just as we were about to set off to the still-unknown location, the car behind started flashing its lights! Thoughts of brick-walled cells and ransom demands flashed through my mind.

I could feel the hitman's legs twitching next to mine, and I could also hear my own heartbeat hammering out a steady dance number in my ears. Suddenly there was a knock on the window. Oliver wound it down to find the hitman's associate stood there staring. He started talking to the hitman in rapid Spanish.

Seconds later, the associate passed a black plastic bag through the window. In the corner of my eye I noticed the hitman place the bag under his right leg, as if he was resting on it. I think everyone feared for the worse. No one knew what it was, but no one was going to question it.

After getting the nod from the hitman, we were back on the road. I found myself trying to think of things to say to make the journey that bit quicker. I knew opening my mouth would only make things worse. You could hear a pin drop and I didn't want to make any sudden movements.

Ten minutes into the journey, I noticed the hitman reach into his right pocket. He pulled out his phone and started scrolling through his pictures. Without making it too obvious I started to look at them out of the corner of my eye. I mean, who could resist?

At first, I didn't see anything untoward. There were family pictures, photos of him in football shirts and shots of him posing next to his friends. But around twenty pictures in, there he was, stood holding a gun. Was he surreptitiously showing me on purpose to intimidate me even more? I couldn't help nudging Amber to get her attention. The atmosphere could have been cut with a knife. There must have been twenty plus pictures of him brandishing his weapon and it felt like he was proud of them all. I think he knew I was looking at the pictures, and he paused a tiny bit at one particular image to let me know who was boss.

The car started to get unbearably hot. I spotted the hitman open the window and place his right hand on the roof grab handle. His t-shirt lifted slightly. There it was, my worst nightmare. A fucking gun tucked under his waistband. My stomach turned. I just wanted to get out of the car for some space, but I knew that wasn't an option.

My heart was pounding and believe me, right around this point in our trip, I was questioning exactly what was wrong with being plied with alcohol on the set of another reality TV programme. Name the bar, the person I had to talk to, hell, I'd even drink a southern lager. If I could have declared 'I'm a Reality TV star, get me out of here' and got my wish, I would.

Two minutes later, the car turned left and into a building that looked like a brothel. Pink bright lights with a sign proclaiming, 'Love Motel' outside lowered my worry setting from 'terrified for my life' to just 'bemused at the current turn of events'. I looked to Amber in disgust.

Oliver continued driving down the long path. I'd been to Amsterdam on several occasions, but this place felt one hundred times seedier. As we drove on a few more metres, we reached a security barrier, which wasn't exactly what I expected at a brothel. Oliver wound down his window to find a concierge button. He pressed the buzzer.

Suddenly I heard a woman reply on the telecom:

'Ola, Cuantas personas?'

Knowing that meant 'How many people' in English, I started to worry about what we were doing at a brothel. It was becoming clear that the interview was planned there.

'Cinco personas,' Oliver replied. Five people.

The line went dead.

Chapter Thirty

A few seconds later, the woman returned. Oliver looked worried. He turned to Johnny, who was sat in the passenger seat and said, 'They will only allow a maximum of four people in each room.'

Instantly I knew there was a problem. There was one too many of us to fit in the love motel. I started to question why it hadn't been pre-organised? There was a decision to be made and it needed to be made fast.

With all the conversation now being spoken in English, I could see the hitman again getting agitated. Oliver looked to Johnny, who decided quickly.

'Sorry guys, the interview is off.'

I was gutted. After the earlier breakdown, the day seemed to be going from bad to worse. Not only had I been sitting in a car with a hitman for thirty minutes, I'd been sitting next to a weapon which I presumed was live. As we reversed back up the driveway, Oliver started chatting with the hitman in Spanish. Oliver turned to Johnny.

'Do you want to try somewhere else? There's a motel a few miles up the road.'

There was a part of me wanted to speak up and say 'No! Enough is enough.' But I also wanted to get the interview done. Amber and I made the decision to continue. After checking that our security were following us in the car behind, we were back on the road. Thunder boomed in the sky and rain began to pour down onto the car. It all seemed to add to the already tense atmosphere.

With the hitman directing Oliver, Johnny made the decision to stop the car. Something just didn't feel right to him. 'Guy's, I think we should head back to our hotel. We don't have a clue where we are heading here. I don't think it's very safe.'

It seemed like a good decision. God knows what the hitman was thinking but, we found ourselves with nowhere to hold the interview. With the rain and thunder still going strong outside there was no chance of finding a random spot. I was still keen to push through the interview, but I hadn't spoken in over thirty minutes. Stupidly, I opened my mouth:

'What about our hotel? Can't we do it there?'

Amber looked at me as if to say, 'Did you actually just suggest that?'

The interview was back on.

Minutes later we were back to square one, our hotel. Amber and I were asked to head upstairs and await further instructions in my room. I couldn't believe the hour we'd just been through. My heart was still thumping, and it took a couple of minutes to shake off the stress of the car journey. When you've been on the edge of your nerves for any time of more than a few minutes, your body starts burning up energy, and I felt like I'd run a half marathon in that hour, not sat in a car next to a Sicario. The first few minutes in the room there was complete silence. I then told Amber about what I'd seen in the car, the reason I was nudging her.

'Did you know he was carrying a gun?'

She laughed nervously; 'What?'

I tried playing it down: 'Yeah, I saw it in his waistband. Surely that's normal for his type of job though?'

She seemed shocked. Knowing she hadn't seen the gun; I made the decision to not tell her about the images I'd seen on the hitman's phone. Maybe it wouldn't have made any difference, but in that moment, she didn't need to hear it.

After thirty minutes nervously waiting in the hotel room, we received a WhatsApp from Johnny.

'If everyone's happy, we are going to do the interview in my room. We are just setting it up now. I'll give you a knock on your rooms shortly for a chat.'

The interview was going ahead. Bringing a hitman back to the hotel probably wasn't the best idea, but the whole team and I were eager to get it done. No one could have written how the night planned out. It seems ludicrous looking back on it but at the time it felt safe!

Again, all sorts of thoughts were rushing through my head. 'What if he comes back at night?', 'Will people have seen him?' and 'Will I get bread and water in my ransom dungeon?'. OK, I wasn't really thinking that last one, but your mind races.

Twenty minutes later Johnny knocked on our door and apologised for the past few hours.

'I know it's been crazy. We are aware that the hitman is carrying a gun, so the agreement is the interview can go ahead on the basis the weapon is kept with his associate outside. Are you two happy with that?'

I looked to Amber and nodded as quickly as you might expect.

'Sitting next to him in a car is a lot worse than this!'

It came as a relief that I wasn't the only one who knew about the weapon.

It would be the first time we'd come face to face with the hitman and look at him directly in the eye. I knew as soon as I entered that interview room and the cameras were on, all the nerves would have to go.

Amber and I slowly walked behind Johnny down the corridor. I'd completely forgotten all my questions that I'd worked so hard on, but I felt ready and focused! After walking no more than ten metres, I entered Johnny's room to find it had been changed into a made-up studio. The crew had flipped his bed onto its side facing upwards and placed it against the wall. The wardrobe was covered up with lighting curtain, and we had to place things to make it look like we weren't in a hotel room.

There was no sign of the hitman. With the room being so small, fitting in the camera equipment, three chairs and the rest of us was a squeeze. The room couldn't have felt any more intense.

'Before we start, lets quickly go through how this is going to work', said Johnny. I could tell even he was nervous. We all wanted it to go smoothly, but for Johnny, all the responsibility fell on his shoulders and it was obvious. His face looked stretched tight with focus and his eyes had a determination that told me that for him, it was an absolute need for everything to go to plan. His plan.

'We should have an hour with the hitman, but if he decides to stop the interview for any reason, then we must respect his decision. As Oliver said before, you can ask pretty much anything. If he doesn't like the question, he will just simply refuse to answer.'

I laughed. 'I don't think you have to worry about any of us questioning his decision to stop the interview.' Johnny continued.

'As you know, the hitman doesn't speak any English so as you have done in previous interviews, direct all questions straight to him, then Oliver will translate after you have finished. He's currently waiting outside with security and his associate so when you're both ready, we'll call him up.'

I just wanted to get it over and done with. I took my seat next to Amber and confidently declared, 'I think we're ready to go!'

Three minutes later, footsteps approached the door and in walked the hitman.

Chapter Thirty-One

He looked a lot smaller than he did in the car. He must have only been around 5ft 8″ and he wasn't the most muscle-bound man I've seen. In fact, he was quite lithe, but then, with the nature of his work, surely that was an advantage if he was to come face to face with a rival gang. I'd have described him as pretty ripped, but normal looking too. I would have easily walked past him on the street never thinking he was a hitman.

I think Colombia is a country with no real recognised 'look' to their inhabitants. As a country, they're vibrant, diverse people, and the Sicario we were meeting would have never stood out in a crowd. Frankly, no Colombian would.

The room was silent. I didn't know how to greet him, but I stuck with a firm handshake and 'Ola.' It was the first time I'd looked him in the eyes in the light. When people say, 'He had the eyes', this was what they were talking about. This man had nothing there. It was like a light had been switched off a long time ago.

As much as I knew what his job was and what he'd done to people, I wanted to show him that little bit of respect for the sake of the interview. He quickly put on a balaclava and spare clothing and sat on the seat parallel to Amber and me. The windows and curtains were closed, and the camera was focused in on us, a tight group of three people. It felt close and way too personal - the hitman sitting inches away.

Even though he was incredibly intimidating, he seemed quite nervous himself, shaky and twitching in his seat. Maybe it was the cameras. I mean, I doubted it was my handshake.

With everyone ready, I opened the interview: 'Hi, firstly thank you for speaking with us. Can you tell me a bit about your job?'

The answer was going to be obvious, but it felt like a good opener. Not only to settle everyone down, but it would be good for the public who'd be watching. If I'd been at home tuning in, I'd want a nice icebreaker; something to ease it in. I didn't expect the answer I got.

'I am a 'Sicario' for the Gulf Cartel.' Sicario was hitman. He had even confirmed the cartel for which he worked. I could have sworn the room's walls closed in a little. Amber was quick to fire back another question to him.

'Can you tell us a bit about how you got into the job?'

'Unfortunately, I didn't choose to be in this position. I went on an excursion and was blackmailed into taking the job.'

'Can you tell us a little more about that?'

'I was away on a trip when gang members from the Gulf Cartel approached me. I was told if I didn't take the position that I would be killed. I had no choice.'

I found it hard to believe that I was sitting no more than three foot away from an active killer. I wanted to make more of a bond with him. That way, I felt he would open up a little more.

'I always dreamed of being a footballer when I was younger. What was your dream job as a child?'

'I always wanted to be a footballer like you!' he giggled. 'Chelsea are my favourite team.'

I suddenly found myself chatting with a hitman about football. I couldn't help disagreeing with this far more serious life choice of which club to support.

'No! Manchester United.' He shook his head in disagreement.

I knew as soon as he answered that question, he felt a little more at ease. Isn't it amazing how football can unite people of all types, in all countries?

'Do you have any family and children?' said Amber.

It was the first time I'd seen a negative reaction. He looked over his shoulder to Oliver for a second, then turned back around to us.

'Yes, I have children. They are the reason I live. This is the only way I can provide for them.'

I swallowed heavily. 'Can you explain how your job works exactly? From start to finish.'

'I usually get a call from my boss. He then sends me a picture. Usually I have two hours to get ready and head out to look for the person. If someone sees him in another area, I will get the call and make my way to the location. Once the person is killed, I take a picture and send it to my boss.'

It all seemed obvious, and he was framing it simply. But it was also just the most unbelievable situation. This man ended people's lives with an eerily casual nature then returned to his wife and kids. It was hard not to look as shocked on screen as I think we were all feeling. Amber asked a question to which everyone wanted the answer.

'How is it you kill them? With a gun? Or a knife?'

'I use a gun. I usually shoot them in the head six times.'

It was at this point that the severity of the person sat in front of me started to sink in. He was clearly a highly dangerous man.

'Are your family aware of your job?' Amber continued.

'No! It's crazy. When I'm back home, my life is totally different. When I leave the house to go to work, they are totally unaware' he told us. I was staggered at the revelation that he had a double life. 'Sometimes I stay away for up to five days.'

I could only imagine the questioning he must have put himself through on a daily basis and it gave us all pause. Despite the tough nature of the answers, the interview was going well.

With the conversation flowing, I tried to understand his thoughts once the so called 'jobs' were done.

'How do you cope, sleeping at night? Do you constantly relive the moment you kill?'

'I do. Sometimes I sit in my car for days thinking about what I have done. I struggle to sleep at night. I usually drive far away from home and I just sit there.'

I couldn't be sure if I was being manipulated or not, but I felt quite sorry for him. It wasn't the fact that he went out killing people to order. The way he had been brought into the gang just seemed unfair. There seemed to be no way out for him.

'What would happen if you were to leave the gang?'

'I couldn't leave. I would be killed instantly. There are around three-thousand active Gulf Cartel members, so there is no way out.' We continued to ramp up the questions.

'How many people have you killed?' Amber asked. No question seemed to bother him.

'I have killed a total of six people. One of them was a very good friend. I didn't want to do it, but I had to.'

All my nerves had dissipated. I'd expected him to say a hundred people, which would have been terrifying, but it only being half a dozen almost made it more real. I could imagine six faces lined up, with big red crosses through them. I wondered if he kept the photos, if he remembered their full names, if he ever thought about them or their devastated families.

Surely, he hadn't made enough money to compensate for the emotional toll of taking multiple lives to order.

'How much do you get paid per kill?' I asked.

'I receive around one million pesos for each hit, and then each month I receive an additional one million.'

Oliver translated those amounts back to us in English. It was worked out that he was paid around three-hundred pounds per kill, and then a further three-hundred monthly. It was hard to believe that someone was getting paid a monthly fee to be on standby waiting to kill. In England, that might be a fortnight's wages pulling pints in a pub.

With the interview coming to a close, there was only time for a few more questions. We needed to bring the subject back to the reason we were there. Drugs.

'What are the main reasons people are killed?' I asked.

'It's usually someone who has stolen from either a drug dealer or a drug house. Mostly theft.'

As the interview wound up, the hitman was passed a bottle of water. My mouth felt that dry that I couldn't even string another sentence together, even if I tried. On camera, we'd come alive, but the magnitude of the night and the incredible, harrowing story he'd told us made me fancy a vodka rather than a water.

Throughout the interview I was in work mode and I stuck at it, but as soon as that camera stopped rolling, and he settled down, I was looking away and I thought that this was the point where he could be volatile.

I felt so privileged to have the chance to do what I was doing, and as the hitman took off his balaclava and wiped his forehead, it was time for Amber and myself to leave and head back to our rooms. I thanked the hitman for his time and walked out rapidly. It had gone a hundred times better than I thought. I just hoped it would look as good on television as it did in person.

The day had been a runaway rollercoaster of an experience. From picking the hitman up, to interviewing him felt like a whirlwind few hours of living in a movie where I had no idea of the ending.

Except it wasn't the end. It was only really the beginning.

Chapter Thirty-Two

The following day, I woke up feeling great. Not only had I successfully interviewed a hitman, but I'd lasted a full six days in Colombia. Morning seemed to be the only time I had to reflect on the journey I'd been on each day. I was still struggling to understand how four young random people had been given the opportunity to meet the people we were meeting. The trip was starting to feel more like a blessing than ever before. I'd travelled five-thousand miles to experience a different world, never thinking that my own world would change as a result, but I'd been wrong - it had affected me on a far deeper level than I would ever have presumed.

Waking up in the new hotel for the first time - and a new city - I was expecting to be given the outline for a tour over breakfast, whatever fruit and egg it might comprise of. But that wasn't the case. Johnny politely informed me that I would be heading out to a town named Turbo, meeting a drug smuggler, and I'd be doing it alone.

With the hitman interview being so intense, another mission under such stressful conditions was the last thing that I'd expected. I sat down with Johnny and discussed the schedule for the day in a little more depth.

'Before we start, I just want to say, yesterday's interview with the hitman was great! Today, you'll be interviewing alone. We have something planned for Amber later in the trip, so that's the reason behind that. When we arrive at the rendezvous point you will hopefully be meeting one of the Gulf Cartel speedboat drivers. He is going to show us a boat similar to one he uses to export cocaine out the country.'

There were many ways I'd imagined cocaine was moved around, by plane, car or person, yet speedboat was easily more fun than any other method of transport, and I couldn't wait to get started. I was also pleasantly surprised and proud about the amount of responsibility they'd given me. It was the first time I'd be interviewing someone on my own and the nerves had returned already, but the previous night's interview had given me a degree of emotional protection from any fear of failure. I had so many questions running through my head, not just for the so-called speedboat driver, but also Johnny. I knew I'd have plenty of time on the way to Turbo to ask them, so I headed back up to my room to prepare.

Just as I was about to jump in the shower, I received a message from Chanel.

'Me and Troi have only just arrived in the South. It's humid as fuck. How are you and Amber coping? We're just about to head into the jungle!'

As much as I wanted to text back telling her the things I'd been up to and the things that had been planned, I made the sensible decision to avoid messaging back. Being in the North wasn't as bad as first expected. Maybe Chanel and Troi were the ones who'd drawn the short straw?

With my mobile phone still in my hand, I decided to Google the Colombian town of Turbo. It was becoming a common theme to research the town to which I was heading. Again, negative results came up. 'Trip from hell!' and 'Don't bother coming to Turbo, Hot and smelly!' were two reviews of the area that stood out.

Twenty minutes later, I was on the coach ready to head a few miles down the road to meet with another mystery stranger, who naturally was involved in the drug trade. I was getting used to filming daily. This time, though, the difference was that all eyes and ears would be fixed only on me.

With Amber joining us on the coach, I decided to ask her if she had thought of any questions for the speedboat driver. She didn't look happy. I wasn't sure if she was pissed off about not interviewing, or she was extremely tired. I decided to presume the latter.

'Ask him what route he uses?' she replied. Maybe she wasn't *that* tired.

Ten minutes before we arrived, I interrogated Johnny. I wanted to know more about the speedboat driver I'd be interviewing, and although I wasn't particularly bothered about the location at which we'd be meeting, because it would be daylight and not the thick darkness of the night. I was more concerned about being driven off on the boat as a hostage or the far likelier possibility that our interview might be intercepted by the police.

'I've met him before. He seems quite calm,' Johnny said with a disarming wave of the hand. 'That may change once we turn up with a load of cameras, but I'm sure we'll be OK. We may be sat on the coach for a while once we arrive. He's due to pick us up on the boat and obviously he can't be waiting around.' I felt a lot calmer than previous days. Surely it couldn't be any more nerve-racking than the night before, when I'd exchanged pleasantries with a professional hitman in Johnny's hotel room?

As we arrived in Turbo, the rain started to fall. It was still incredibly humid. I knew if there was any chance of the interview going ahead the rain would have to stop! Expensive cameras and water don't mix well. Turbo itself was clearly a port city, with boats everywhere and a general feel of somewhere that many people moved through, but few would travel to as a permanent destination.

I looked out of the coach window for a place a drug smuggler would enter or depart, but it was almost impossible. The town was full of shops, motorbikes and tightly packed houses, and even though the coach doors were shut, and we were inching our way through traffic, all we could smell was fish. There didn't seem to be anything appealing about Turbo.

Suddenly, the coach pulled up to an empty beach. I was confused about why we'd stopped, so I asked Johnny.

'We'll hang around here until Oliver gets the nod.' As we waited, the clouds cleared, and the sun came out. From afar, the beach might have looked like Blackpool on a good day, although in Turbo, they weren't quite so used to British people arriving on cue on a big white coach. We were far from discreet.

With the heat intensifying, I needed some fresh air, but getting off the coach alone was a no-go according to Oliver, and I didn't mind being restricted this time. It didn't feel like a place you would want to stroll around on your own, especially as a tourist. The beach was ramshackle to say the least, with donkeys and people meandering through huts and palms in the heat.

After ten minutes waiting patiently, the crew made the decision to get off the coach and head over to the beach. There seemed to be some spare time, so the cameraman decided to film some walk-in shots. My every move being filmed was becoming normal and, as tired as I was, I was loving every minute of it.

Just a few minutes later, I found myself relaxing in a chair on the beach, in the middle of one of Colombia's most dangerous towns, which felt quite surreal. With Amber not interviewing anyone, she was lapping up the sun next to me.

An hour passed, and there was still no contact with the speedboat driver. I was getting worried that the interview would be called off. Suddenly, I spotted two men in the distance walking towards us. With the beach empty, it felt slightly odd. The closer they got to us, the more I started to question who they were. The guy I was due to interview was supposed to be on a boat, not strolling down the beach.

They must have got to within twenty metres of us before Amber turned to me.

'Is that the guy from last night, the hitman's associate?'

Chapter Thirty-Three

What the fuck was he doing here? Had something happened last night? It looked like him, but I wasn't sure. Oliver started to walk towards them. He started speaking to them, again in Spanish. I'd never been so interested in finding out what was being said between other people.

I wished I could lip-read, but without that skill, I was resigned to watching and waiting. I tried to read their body language, and as Oliver seemed to know everyone in Colombia, I began to calm down. If things weren't fine, he'd have let us know. After twenty minutes of them chatting and me relaxing Oliver came over and explained the situation.

'OK, we're going to make our way to the location now. My friend here is going to show us the way. Is everyone ready?'

I'd completely got the wrong end of the stick, and it was at that point I realised Oliver's so-called friend was more like a local fixer. The man who had the contacts to all the dangerous criminals. He didn't really talk much to us and seemed very business-like, yet we respected him and twenty-minutes later, we arrived at the location. It was only a short drive from the beach, but the roads were that bumpy it felt like I'd been on a two-hour journey.

As I stepped off the coach, I spotted a long narrow boat in the distance heading towards the shore. There were two people on it, the driver and a man with his back turned to us. I looked to Johnny.

'If that is the boat, there is no way all six of us are fitting on that!'

It looked cheap and wasn't what I expected from a gang who were making millions exporting cocaine.

As the boat came ever closer, the cameraman started offloading the equipment from the coach. That was the point I knew there was no going back, and this was the man we were waiting for. While both men remained onboard, Oliver started talking with the local fixer again. There seemed to be some confusion about how it was going to work. The associate wanted to conduct the interview on dry land, but the director wanted to do it out on the boat at sea. The conversation seemed to be getting slightly heated, so with Amber still sat on the coach, I decided to stay out of the way and join her.

In the end, four of us were allowed onto the boat. Johnny and I would board with Oliver and one cameraman. It made sense, and after all the confusion Johnny was confident that the interviewee could be pushed, with all questions permissible.

'They'll take us out on the boat, showing us some of the routes they use to export the cocaine, and then finally we will stop off and do a short interview. Believe it or not he seems quite friendly, so don't be afraid to ask him anything.' Said Johnny.

I couldn't quite believe I was about to get on a speedboat which was used to export cocaine. The questions were flooding through my head. The main one being where they might store the drugs.

I quickly said goodbye to Amber, left the coach and headed towards the boat. Everything felt quite relaxed. With some of the crew staying behind, I decided to leave all my belongings with them. I then put one leg overboard but found myself struggling. The speedboat man grabbed my hand and kindly helped me. That was my first interaction with him. I'm not sure if he knew I was the one interviewing him, but he was being overly polite. Everywhere I'd been in Colombia seemed to be the same, no matter if they were criminals or not. As there were no seats, I perched on the edge, my bottom clinging onto the side of the boat mostly by willpower. The cartel driver spoke to us while his associate took the wheel, and we pulled away from the small docking area and into open water.

Worried that the cameras were rolling, the speedboat driver immediately asked for protection over his face. It looked like he already had a balaclava, but he was worried that wasn't enough to cover his eyes. Stupidly, I offered him my RayBan sunglasses to wear. He was quite happy to accept, and I half-wondered if they might ever make their return.

As we made our way out to sea, there was a weird atmosphere. All I could hear was the boat engine running and it seemed like we were the only vessel at sea. I was expecting police and military to be spot-checking the area, but it was deserted, and you could have seen them a mile off.

Without warning the boat suddenly started to speed up. At that point, the driver and interviewee told the crew to put all the cameras down. He quickly pulled off the balaclava and turned his head towards us.

'Tranquilo, Tranquilo!' He shouted.

'Oliver, what's going on?' I said, panicking.

'Everyone stay calm.' Oliver translated quickly.

I noticed a boat in the distance heading towards us. It looked very similar to the one we were in. With the lack of communication, I wasn't sure if it was a rival gang, the police or that he just wanted everyone to relax. The speedboat parted the water as it roared towards us and drew closer.

Chapter Thirty-Four

Two minutes passed, and everyone was still and silent. Anyone looking at us from a distance would have immediately noticed that we were a camera crew out filming with someone dodgy. Luckily the boat passed with no issues. It just illustrated the tenseness of the whole environment. Every hiccup seemed to be huge and caused a look of panic to dart between everyone on board who wasn't Colombian.

As we made our way further out to sea, I was then shown the different routes the drivers would take if they were shipping cocaine out of the country. Not that I would remember them, but they seemed to be very distinct areas, as if they had been purposely cornered off for smugglers only. Each location was very narrow with plenty of cover.

With the boat going slowly to attract less attention, it had taken us over thirty minutes to reach the border points. It was time to head back towards the harbour and conduct the interview. There was still a little bit of confusion as to whether it would be taking place on dry land or water. Obviously from a TV perspective, Johnny, who was directing, wanted it out at sea. The only thing I was worried about was that the only means of escape should my subject take objection to the questions I put to him, would be overboard!

Johnny made the call to do the interview out at sea. Now the pressure started to build. All the questions had made their way out of my head and I had around twenty minutes to think while we made our way back to Turbo. There was little conversation between anyone. Obviously, the language barrier was a big issue. There's nothing worse than a group talking and you not knowing what they're saying, especially in that type of situation.

As the boat drew to a stop, the engines remained running. Everything around us was so calm. The water, the trees on land and now not a cloud in the sky. Johnny asked me to sit directly opposite the speedboat driver and rest on the side of the boat facing inwards, with the sea to my back. The cameras started to roll. I opened the interview again with the fairly obvious question a viewer might ask.

'So, can you tell me about your job? What is it you do?'

I found it very hard to look at him directly in the eye, not because I wasn't confident enough, just because he had my RayBan sunglasses back on! I knew it was going to be difficult to get any sort of emotion out of a person with a yellow bright head scarf covering his face and shades on, so the answers would tell all.

'I am a driver for the Gulf Cartel. I mainly use boats to export cocaine out of the country.'

I found it hard to believe that someone using the type of boat we were on would have the audacity to even try fleeing with huge quantities of cocaine. But what type of boat was it and why choose that one?

'It may not look very fast,' he said with a smile, 'but believe me, if the police get behind me, I say, "Bye Bye".

I found it hard not to smirk. I was in disbelief at how relaxed he seemed about the whole thing if the police were to chase him. It appeared that the Gulf Cartel had the upper hand. I wanted to ask a little more.

'So, you're telling me, if you were ever to be chased by the police you would be able to speed off without getting caught?'

He replied 'Yes, but it's not that simple. The police, Navy and border control also carry weapons, so sometimes we may get into gun fire. This is the last thing we want.'

Gunfire and boats circling drop-offs might look the business on Miami Vice, but it wasn't a show I fancied starring in.

'There are so many people involved,' he continued, 'and I am just one of the many people who will be in contact with the drugs whilst exporting. It will usually be delivered to a location point where I or my associate will then go and pick up. We are then responsible to deliver it to the next location, which in our case is usually another country. After that, it has nothing to do with me.'

I found it hard to believe that a small narrow boat, half the size of a canal boat back home would be able to reach another country, let alone while presumably being stocked to the gills with several kilograms of cocaine. There had to be somewhere to store it, and it had to be well hidden. It just didn't look like there was any spare room onboard?

'Sometimes we will put it on the deck and pack things over it. Other times, it is stored under the boat.' Under the boat? I didn't understand.

'Sometimes it is welded to the bottom of the boat. Obviously, this is a lot harder to transport as the cocaine must be fully waterproofed. It also involves a lot more work.'

These people certainly knew what they were doing. Everybody we'd interviewed in the North up to that point had all been linked to the Gulf Cartel, the same gang that Oliver had mentioned when we were eating during the first few days.

'The Gulf Cartel are bigger than any cartel Colombia has ever had'. Oliver had said.

After being told how the drugs came onboard and were transported elsewhere, I grilled the driver about whether he knew the route to Britain.

'Yes, Britain is a very popular destination for the drug, but it is a little too far for me to know the routes taken. I would imagine it is imported in to Britain from Spain.'

I then went into the price of cocaine at its source and how much he was paid for doing the job he did. While I'd felt like the hitman was now in a career that he would struggle to ever retire from, the speedboat driver struck me as someone who had decided for himself the life he led.

He did mention how his home was completely trashed from a previous storm and that enticed him to want to continue smuggling, but everyone who was involved in the trade seemed to have not an excuse, but a reason as to why they had got into their jobs. He told me that he makes around two million pesos per drop. That was the equivalent to five-hundred pounds. He wouldn't go into too much detail about the amounts he was smuggling each time, but I'd imagined a lot! It was very close to the amount the hitman received. I know which job I'd have preferred doing.

The interview was going great. He seemed to be telling me everything I wanted to know without me even having to ask. He even questioned me on a few things. He asked me about the quality of cocaine once it arrives in the UK. I told him that a single gram of cocaine in the UK cost around forty pounds. His response was simply a giggle. 'That's around fifteen times the price if you were to buy it here, right?' I looked around as if to say, 'You tell me.'

Before long, the interview was complete, and everyone was incredibly pleased with how it had gone. The cameraman told me that it was one of the best interviews he'd ever sat in on. I was buzzing.

As each interview passed, I was growing in confidence. Most of the people I'd met from the criminal world seemed to be down to earth people who had just been caught up at a bad time and fallen into the wrong job. Back in the UK, there are all sorts of ways that the government help its citizens regarding benefits or schemes to help people gain a job. In Colombia, there seemed to be nothing.

It was time to head back to the hotel. I wanted to find out a bit more from Oliver about what life is like for the rich in

Colombia. I'd seen one side of the country, but surely not all parts of it were the same?

'Colombia is blessed with many minerals and energy resources. The country has significant amounts of gold and silver. There are many wealthy people here. Most of them are involved in real estate properties and banking.' Said Oliver.

It was hard to imagine what life would be like for the rich living there. I suppose in any country you have the good and bad areas and it's how you look at it. I wanted to know more but I knew that the trip wasn't about the rich and famous. It was about discovering the underworld of cocaine.

As we pulled up into the hotel carpark, around twenty military guards were spread evenly lined up against the hotel front, all of them armed and looking like they meant business. Nothing shocked me at this point, but I immediately panicked, thinking that it might be something to do with us taking the hitman back to our hotel the night before. Suddenly, Oliver jumped off the coach.

'Wait here a minute while I speak with them.'

Two minutes later he arrived back. Oliver told us that the military were there to guard the hotel as they had some Chinese officials visiting the area. Most likely it was something to do with the millions of bananas in the fields across the road. We got the all-clear to enter the hotel. I was happy to be back on solid ground but was still on an emotional high about the interview. I was pleased with the job I'd done and still buzzing with energy after the whole experience. That interview in particular is something I'm looking forward to watching with the family. I think they will be extremely proud.

Having only been in the North of Colombia for just under two days, I was already seeing the differences between the areas of the country. Medellín seemed to be a lot more touristy whereas Apartadó and Turbo were places you wouldn't dare visit on a family holiday.

That being said, there were a few restaurants nearby which Oliver wanted to try out. After quickly changing we were back on the coach ready to head a couple of hundred metres down the road to a local seafood restaurant. I'd never been a fan of fish really, only fish fingers as a child. Safe to say, I wasn't looking forward to the meal ahead.

As we sat down to dinner, Johnny revealed that we would be staying in the North a little longer. It was the news I'd been waiting for since I started the show.

'Tomorrow we will be meeting up with the military. Unfortunately, we have no idea what is planned for us yet, only to remain on standby for early morning. You can probably understand the reason for that. I'm sure they don't want us letting any secrets out.'

I looked to Amber sat opposite, who gazed like a child on Christmas morning. My face lit up. I had a vision of us heading out in a helicopter on a mission trying to catch the gangsters, but I knew that was very unlikely. The most I was expecting was to be driven around the camp, maybe shown a few guns, but this was a whole lot more. The night ended sooner than we might have planned, but there was a feeling growing in my stomach as I fell asleep awaiting what the next day would bring.

Chapter Thirty-Five

Since arriving in Colombia, I'd only really met and interviewed people who were either involved in the criminal side of producing, exporting or selling cocaine, or those who used it. It was going to be the first time I'd be meeting and interviewing the people who were doing their best to put a stop to the spread of the drug, and it was the day I'd been waiting for. We were about to meet the military!

Oliver had briefed us the night before, and he told us that gaining access to filming with the military was unprecedented. I was up at 6am and raring to go. I still wasn't sure on how the day would pan out. In my head, we'd be in helicopters, sweeping up some of the drug smugglers that had fascinated us throughout our trip. Was it the end game for the Gulf Cartel?

Before we met them, I must admit I'd been feeling slightly guilty about my previous interactions with some of the people they were probably trying to catch. I'd sat down with a hitman and a getaway driver of a speedboat. Both collars would have been huge ones to take for the Colombian military who we were about to meet.

We were told that after we'd had breakfast, Amber and I would have to pack an overnight bag in case we ended up staying at the military camp we'd be visiting. I wasn't particularly keen on staying overnight at another different location, but at least we'd be safer there than probably anywhere else in Colombia, so I did as I was told. If we did end up staying, it was best to be prepared. I just couldn't imagine what a bed would be like in a Colombian military camp.

One hour later we were driven to Apartadó police station, totally clueless as to what the next day or two would bring. As we arrived, we were met by police waiting at the front gates. Mirrors were placed on the floor so that the guards could see under our coach, checking for any type of explosives or weapons. Minutes later we were invited in and told by the Commander to wait outside in the main gardening area until further notice.

While it was a police station by name, it was also a military base, a quite different set-up to the army and police in Britain. It was also an operations' base, and the mission was to stop the cartels. Military and police alike were pulling in the same direction. It felt slightly strange that the same town I was at the day before to interview a smuggler was now the police base for an operation investigating the people I'd been asked to speak to about their life and work.

Suddenly, a helicopter started to circle above. Surely that wasn't going to be our lift to the military camp. But sure enough, the helicopter landed in the field right in front of us and out stepped four soldiers while the pilot remained on board. They signalled for us to come over to get into the helicopter.

At this point, I wasn't alone in staring, flabbergasted at the whole scene. I'd never been on a helicopter, so to hear the propellers spinning and seeing four soldiers armed for war made me feel like I was in a dream. Johnny being a quick thinker shouted, 'Amber, Louis, you go ahead. I will film you entering the helicopter.'

I quickly ran towards it in excitement. The helicopter was huge and easily held all of us, and as the soldiers in charge strapped me and Amber in on opposite sides facing outwards with the door open, we gazed out at the land around us, aware that it would soon be disappearing from view. They then shouted Johnny and Oliver over and did the same for them.

With Johnny and Oliver seated next to me, I had no idea how Amber was feeling. Looking at Johnny's face I could see he was worried. I think it was to do with the fact he was holding a fifty-thousand-pound camera in his hand about to

175

set off in a helicopter with the doors wide open! As the propellers started to spin faster, we started to rise. The feeling of a helicopter taking off is something that will live with me forever, despite the fact there was a gun being manned by one of the soldiers. He pointed it at the area below the helicopter as we rose.

We were off, gunsight swinging left and right, scanning the area below us as we ascended. As we travelled to Turbo in style at a few thousand feet, from the air, Colombia looked nearly as green and as pleasant as England itself. The foliage was denser and the pockets of jungle, dirt tracks and banana fields replaced more familiar sights to this Mancunian's eyes such as motorways, high-rises and football grounds, but it was no less picturesque.

Sitting in a helicopter with the doors open travelling at such a high speed was a feeling like no other. With the guns hanging from the side of the helicopter, I felt like I was shooting a movie. The sound of the blades spinning around and around was the noisiest thing I'd ever heard, but I didn't care. I could have travelled in a helicopter all day. There was a constant buzz and crackle of chatter on the soldiers' radio walkie-talkies. Everyone was on high alert.

Twenty minutes later after dashing across the sky, we were at the military camp. As the helicopter landed safely, the sound of the propellers was still ringing in my ears. I couldn't help noticing the huge vehicles and number of helicopters parked up ready to go.

As Amber, Johnny, Oliver and I made our way across the tarmac helipad we were greeted by a junior soldier. Although they were the first military personnel on the ground, there seemed to be a real presence about them.

'Welcome, thank you for joining us. If you follow me, I will show you to the general's office. He is expecting you.'

I don't know if you've ever been a civilian on an army base, but if you have, you'll know that in the UK at least, the army don't have any control over what non-Army personnel (as you would be called) get up to. They can't order you around, you don't have to salute them, and their power is effectively null and void. But in Colombia, the respect the army soldiers have for their superiors is such that you almost snap into a salute as a 'civvy'. I certainly wasn't sitting with my hands in my pockets. Oliver seemed to be in his element whilst Amber, Johnny and I looked stunned.

After being shown into the general's office we sat in silence for a good few minutes. Colombian flags adorned the walls, and we sat in wide, comfortable chairs. This was no soldiers mess room. I got the feeling that we were meant to be impressed by the surroundings of the general, and I was sure that any soldiers called to that room would have been extremely nervous. The theme was power, and it was impossible to miss.

I felt like I was sat in a waiting room pending a job interview. Suddenly, in walked the general. 'Ola'. He had the patriarchal aura about him of a head teacher. I didn't know whether to stand up and shake his hand or remain seated and let Oliver do the talking. I chose to nod my head and say 'hello' in his mother tongue by way of respect.

As expected, the general only spoke in Spanish so it was down to Oliver again. Totally clueless as to what was being said, I was waiting for a gap in the conversation to get an update. I was excited to find out what was planned for the day ahead.

Ten minutes later the conversation came to a halt. The general stood up off his seat and said 'Gracias.' I looked to Amber, 'Is that it?' I thought that was going to be the last we saw of him until I saw Oliver's face light up. I knew there was some good news waiting.

Amber, Johnny and I looked to Oliver desperate to find out. 'Ok so the plan for today…' I couldn't wait much longer, 'Spit it out Oliver' … 'Firstly we will be sitting in on a meeting with one of the chief intelligence officers. They will explain how the operation works, who their key targets are and finally they will show us some of their success stories. They will then explain a bit about the history of the operation. Then hopefully... fingers crossed we will be heading out with a squad on a mission. Again, by helicopter.'

After several minutes sat nervously waiting, the intelligence officer walked into the general's office. I couldn't quite believe the access we were getting.

'Please follow me' he said. Johnny, Amber, Oliver and I made our way single file towards the meeting room. I was in total shock as to where I was.

Shortly after taking a seat in the meeting room, Johnny asked if it was OK to film the brief.

'No, no, no' came the vocal from the soldiers. Understandably, as part of the intelligence sector of the Colombian military, they were worried for their anonymity.

Once the brief started, I felt clueless again, due to everything being in Spanish. I had to ask Oliver if he could translate what was being said after every break in speech. I could see the soldiers getting frustrated as they were there to do a job. The chief intelligence officer then started pointing at the TV with several faces on it, explaining how the operation worked and who were their key targets.

As the brief continued, it was interesting to hear from the other side of the drugs trade. From a military perspective, Colombian intelligence believed that between 2015 and 2018 they had brought down over two-thousand cartel members. I found that very hard to believe, but the pictures they had on the walls seemed to prove it, with many of the manacled men who had been captured being leaders.

I couldn't work out how they would ever stop the drugs trade completely. Was their ultimate goal simply restricting the success of their enemies, or did they really believe that they could bring the entire drugs trafficking industry down like a pack of cards?

After several questions, we established that the main leader of the Gulf Cartel was still out there somewhere in Colombia, they just didn't know where. One thing that stuck out from the meeting was being told how the cartels rarely use any sort of communication. They'd only be in contact when absolutely necessary, which made it very hard to track them down, as well as the fact that they had over two-hundred lookouts spread across the North of the country. Apparently, each time a helicopter or vehicle left the military camp, the cartel members would be the first to know. Were more of the cartels watching the police, or the authorities watching the criminals? The whole meeting had left me with more questions than answers, but I'd found it fascinating.

After being escorted back to the general's office, we took our familiar seats to wait yet again. We'd been in the camp around two hours, but it felt like five minutes. Seconds later, the door opened. It was the general. After talking to Oliver for a while, he relayed the message back to us in English.

'Shortly, we will be heading out on a mission. Please follow me to the briefing room.'

My heart sunk. It was exactly what I'd been waiting for. Johnny was obviously buzzing from a TV perspective too. I could see in Oliver's eyes he was happy. As a fixer, it was exactly what he wanted, and we certainly felt excited about the afternoon ahead!

As we made our way to the briefing room, the general took us on a quick tour guide of the camp. I couldn't believe the number of vehicles parked up, from powerful helicopters to armoured cars. The number of soldiers spread around the camp, all there to crack down on this one gang, the Gulf Cartel, was amazing. I was intrigued to see which vehicle we would be heading out in, but I was guessing it wasn't one of the two black hawk helicopters parked up.

Everyone seemed very happy to see us, as if they were showing their might and control over the area, demonstrating their power via the medium of television.

After a quick tour, I found myself in another meeting room, again totally clueless as to what was being said. The general stood at the front of the room waving his hand at several points on the Colombian map. He explained how we would head out by helicopter in search of any signs of illegal activity on the ground in areas often used by cartel members. They were mainly on the lookout for communication centres, places the gangs would use to speak directly with each other, or even plan their next moves. Information was the biggest weapon in the war on drugs and they quickly got us geared up ready to go on a military exercise.

I looked around to Amber sat next to me in complete shock. 'Wait, what? We're actually going out on a mission now?'

Oliver replied instead.

'Yes, but don't worry, there will be thirty soldiers joining us, so hopefully there shouldn't be too much to worry about.'

The number of soldiers joining us wasn't my worry; I was more concerned that the helicopter might be shot at. What would happen if we found some active cartel members? Even worse, what if we found one of the very people we'd been speaking with over the past few days? It was highly unlikely, but I didn't fancy asking for my RayBan sunglasses back from a suspect as the police were collaring him. It's a small world out there.

As I stepped out of the dark briefing room into the bright sun, I was still in a state of shock. I couldn't help focusing my attention on the two Black Hawk helicopters parked up only metres away. Surely, they wouldn't allow us to use them?

Minutes earlier I'd been told that Colombian police are the only police in the world to own and use Black Hawk helicopters, and there were two of them! They meant business.

Minutes later, I spotted Oliver and Johnny in the distance talking intensely to the General. Oliver then relayed it back to Amber and me as we waited patiently in the scorching heat.

'Ok guys, I've been told to go over a few rules with you. Whilst out in the helicopters, there could be a chance that we come under fire. There is always a risk to going out on a live mission, but this is the stuff we've been waiting for, right?'

Amber and I nodded in agreement. Oliver continued; 'Whilst out in the helicopters and on the ground, there will be several soldiers who will be looking after us. Please always follow and listen to them. They are the ones in charge whilst on the mission.

'From a TV side of things,' said Johnny, 'Try to enjoy it. There will be times where you may feel slightly nervous, but I'm sure we'll be absolutely fine. We are in great hands!'

Suddenly, on went the bulletproof kit, metal helmet and we were all attired in uniform before you could say 'attention!'.

Watching thirty soldiers walking in a line towards the helicopters was a picture. At the time it almost didn't feel real. What an earth is a young lad from Manchester doing heading out on a live mission with the Colombian military? Safe to say my head was all over the place.

As we reached the helipad, the soldier in charge made sure we had our choice of which helicopter in which to travel. Of course, we all chose the Black Hawk. I'm not sure how many people they hold, but it was a beast!

With all three helicopters joining us on the mission, it almost felt like they were putting a statement out to the cartels announcing their arrival. The sounds of three sets of propellers preparing for take-off was almost deafening.

With the bulletproof gear weighing me down in the intense heat, I almost felt like one of the soldiers.

As we entered the chopper, I couldn't help noticing the organisation of the military. Although they probably do those types of things daily, every action was done to a routine.

I could barely see outside. The helicopter was packed! Amber, Johnny and Oliver all squeezed in next to me. Without a seat, I found myself crouched down holding on to a small rope hanging from the roof. We were ready for take-off.

With the whole trip mostly being on impulse I found myself yet again totally clueless as to what was going on. Everything happened so quickly. I'd been advised in the briefing that a certain soldier would be looking after us, both in the helicopter and on the ground, but there was no stand out man. Without any sort of weapon, I was helpless if something was to kick off. I felt like an open target.

As we made our ascent, an order came through to the helicopter telling us that the squadron was needed elsewhere. Suddenly, the chopper swung left and banked away from our intended target.

We were on the move and I had no idea to where.

Chapter Thirty-Six

If there was any time to start panicking, it was now. However, I felt slightly better after being reassured by the soldiers looking after us that it was quite normal to be called elsewhere whilst out on a mission. We were heading to an active cartel sighting just twenty miles away. With the Black Hawk helicopters travelling at one-hundred and seventy-five mph, I knew we were only a matter of minutes away.

As the propellers continued to roar, I couldn't hear myself speak. I was trying to get Johnny's attention to see if it was part of the plan. But communication was impossible, and I was forced to wait impatiently to arrive at the unknown destination, totally clueless as to what the next hour of my life would bring.

Suddenly, the propellers started to slow down, and as the two helicopters following side by-side began to circle around us, I knew we were going to be first to descend. With guns being pointed at the ground from both sides of the chopper, we had a slight advantage over anyone who would dare try shooting at us, though the mission no longer felt like TV. This was real life, and it was hurtling towards us as fast as our descending Black Hawk helicopter.

From the gaps between soldiers, I could see that we were landing in a very open area. It reminded me of the countryside back in the UK. It was just as green, yet almost certainly not as pleasant. There was the odd house and a scattering of haystacks. It wasn't a place I could imagine cartels hiding out. There was a lot being said over the radio, between soldiers in the air and on the ground, and from what I could make out, everything was being taken very seriously.

We must have dropped to within two-hundred feet of the marked location when I finally made eye contact with Johnny.

'What happens once we land?'

'Just follow the soldier in charge,' he shouted over the din. 'The one beside you. He will take care of you.'

The nerves started to kick in.

The helicopter landed almost immediately, and I had no time to think about anything else. The doors were slammed open and all I heard was the bellow of 'Venga, Venga!'. People of a certain age might associate that cry with a 1990's dance party song, but not the soldiers onboard the Black Hawk. They exited the helicopter quicker than I could say 'Cartel member at 3 o'clock', and none of them were waiting for the Vengabus. They stalked off towards the location, pointing their weapons at the target area with focused intensity. The place they were heading towards looked like an old shack, but the area was in the open, so everyone was on high alert for any sort of movement up ahead.

We finally got the all clear and it was time for Amber, me and the rest of the crew to be escorted from the helicopter. While Johnny was trying to do his best to film anything he could, the rest of us found ourselves crouching across the field as instructed by the man in charge, backs bent and faces looking at the ground as the wind whipped the air directly above our heads.

Around ten soldiers stood in a symmetrical line in front of us, all crouched down. One of the helicopters above then started to make its descent, dropping off more soldiers. When I met up with Oscar in the slums earlier in the journey, I had said that the trip felt like 'Call of Duty'. I'd been wrong, but only because this new mission really was like that game, but in real life. This all felt way too real and intense, and the atmosphere was such that everyone was focused on one aim, namely getting what we had come for and staying alive in the process. It was army life in microcosm, the relentless routine and hours of training all going towards short, intense periods of extreme concentration and a collective focus on a single objective. It was both fascinating and literally awesome to watch it happening around me.

Seconds after we'd left the chopper, there were thirty soldiers on the ground. As we made our way slowly across the muddy fields, I felt like I was at war. Although I couldn't see anybody up ahead, there was a feeling that any sort of movement would have triggered action in the field. I could hear snippets of Spanish being whispered between the soldiers. With the helicopters circling above ready for our immediate evacuation, I was ready to go a little further.

I found a moment to ask the soldier; 'Why is it that we're here? What are we looking for?'

'We have been told by intelligence on the ground that this house has been used for communication very recently', he responded whilst breathing heavily, 'We have come to check it out.'

On we went through the thick mud. As we approached the 'casa', we were advised by the soldiers ahead that the cartels had fled the scene, probably after hearing the helicopters as they dropped down into their patch.

I was keen to have a look inside the property, but I wasn't allowed. Even though it was given the all clear, there was potentially evidence that wasn't to be touched. Apparently, they'd found telephone numbers and contacts of people working there. I found that very hard to believe. Maybe we'd been told that, so the mission didn't appear to have been pointless, but I went along with it. I then heard the roar of the helicopters fly back over us. It was time to head back to the military camp.

A short while later, we were back on the ground, safe and sound. I felt like I'd just finished playing a video game and returned to reality. Although I didn't hear any gunfire, walking through an area where there's a high possibility of that happening is almost as terrifying as being eliminated first in a *Battle Royale*. We were all still standing, so nobody had lost.

Travelling in so many helicopters in one day almost made it feel like the only mode of transport. Everything they showed us, from the mission control to the intelligence briefing and then the cartel location proved how much hard work goes into stopping the Colombian cocaine trade, and, to an extent, how fruitless a mission can feel on a day-to-day basis.

As I pulled off my body armour, I felt drained. I wasn't sure if the sun had got to my head, but I felt dizzy. I needed a rest, a drink, a sit down. I then started to feel trapped, homesick, restless and as much as I had enjoyed the day, I just wanted to leave.

It was easy to forget that for the soldiers who were in the helicopter with us, they would be going out on another mission very soon, and again and again, fighting what must sometimes feel like an endless series of missions to stop the tide of drugs sweeping across the nation.

But knowing our hotel was either a twenty-minute helicopter ride or a one-hour car journey away, I had to stick out the rest of the day. My worst nightmare at that stage then happened. We were informed by Oliver that we would be staying overnight.

It was probably one of the only times in the whole journey where I just needed my own space and my own bed. I'd never thought of joining the military, probably because I wouldn't be mentally strong enough, but I respected everything they'd done and shown us, so I agreed to carry on.

It was time for dinner, another part of the day I wasn't looking forward to. As we walked into the food hall packed full of soldiers, I was expecting an unfriendly welcome but that wasn't the case, although that may have been helped by the fact we were going to be joined by the general at our table.

I knew if the food was going to be anything like I'd imagined South American military food to look like, then I would be in for an awkward meal ahead. I didn't want to be the disrespectful one who ended up leaving it all, but it was all starting to go a little like Indiana Jones and his misadventures at the Temple of Doom, trying to convince his fellow adventurer to eat what they were given. What was to come out of the kitchen in the next ten minutes was crucial.

Let's just say, it didn't start well. With no option of what to drink, I received a glass of banana juice. Of course, banana juice. With the hundreds of banana fields just miles down the road it made perfect sense. I just couldn't quite explain the stale chips, hard rice and piece of chicken I'd been handed on a plate. As I picked at the chips one-by-one I couldn't help looking around to see how much everyone else had eaten. It wasn't much, so I was pleased.

The conversation over dinner was as scarce as the flavour and tenderness in our meal. That seemed to be the case across the thirty tables spread across the food hall. I wanted to know the plan for the evening. We'd been out on a mission, we'd seen the intelligence side, what more was to be seen?

The short answer was... nothing. Not long after dinner we'd been told there wasn't anything planned for the evening. Although it was 7pm and I wasn't feeling great, there was no way I was falling asleep at that time. I decided to ask Johnny if we could nip to the shop outside of the base, totally unaware that one of the senior soldiers was standing behind me. Luckily, he spoke English. 'I will take you; we will take the car.'

The sense of relief was huge! Although I was only leaving for a matter of minutes, I just needed that small break away from everything and everyone - even if that was thanks to telling a small lie, that I needed a new toothbrush from the shop.

A while later, I was back in camp and being shown to my room for the night by the senior soldier. I had no idea what a Colombian military camp bed would be like. I'd imagined sleeping next to thirty men with no room to breathe or fart, but that wasn't the case. I was joined by Amber, Johnny and Oliver and we'd been given the general's apartment block which was located on camp for himself and any visiting family. I was buzzing. Not only did I have my own room and shower, I had a TV!

Knowing I had to be up at the crack of dawn, I dosed off to the sounds of the Colombian news being played through the TV. It was probably one the best night's sleep I'd had since arriving in Colombia and I woke up feeling a lot fresher than I did the day before.

Johnny had knocked on my door at 7am and we ate breakfast at the food hall - a hard poached egg and stale bread were offered, but I stuck to the packet of crisps I'd bought in the shop the night before.

'The plan for today is obviously dependent on the general and what he wants to do with us. We've covered lots of things visually, but I would like you two to sit down with him and have a face to face interview, something a little more formal.'

As if by coincidence, the General arrived, and out of instinct, I hid my crisps under the table. Amber started smirking. Knowing he only spoke Spanish, I was worried that when he started chatting with Oliver, he'd be telling him to tell me off, but that wasn't the case.

'He is happy to be interviewed formally,' Oliver told us. 'The interview will be stopped at any time he likes. This one is going to be a bit more difficult, so do hold back with the more negative questions.'

188

We then spoke to the General in a room packed with pictures of captured cartel members plastered all over the wall. Being a higher rank in the military, I imagined he had already done media before, so the interview would flow nicely, and true enough, when Amber asked him what life was like for his soldiers living on base fighting the cartels on missions away, we received a polished reply.

'I would be lying if I said it wasn't tough. We must be prepared for anything. The people we are fighting against are very dangerous, so each day is never the same.'

I wanted to understand if and how buying and selling cocaine in the UK affected the operation. It was, after all, the trail that had led us to him.

'Lots of cocaine is produced in Colombia, but each time someone contributes to the cycle of buying and selling, no matter where, it makes our jobs a lot more difficult. Whilst there are high demands for the drug, people will want to make money from it.'

If I was a general of the military and I had a production company filming about the very thing they were clamping down on, I would be asking the presenters all sorts of questions, like who we'd met, what we'd found out, but he didn't seem to care too much about that. I wondered whether that was because the problem was so rife that a few people were of next to no value to him in the grand scheme of his operation. It could just as easily have been out of pride, however. He wanted another picture on his wall, and not in our programme. They were the ones tasked with bringing in the drug dealers, exporters and everyone who worked in that chain.

Amber closed out the interview asking him whether he thought the military would ever be able to close down the cocaine trade completely, but he refused to answer and off came the microphone tied around his neck in one swift move. The interview was over and so was the morning. It was time to gather our belongings from the rooms and head to the General's office yet again.

After some discussion between Oliver and the officers in charge, it was revealed that we'd be heading out with the Navy. We'd be shown some of their operation and then head back to Apartadó later in the day.

By this stage nothing shocked me. After thanking the General and his soldiers for showing us around the camp and telling us about his life fighting against the cartels, we were back on one of the Black Hawk helicopters ready to head to Turbo's port, the home of the Navy.

Travelling by helicopter almost felt like a taxi service and it must have been the sixth ride of the trip. God knows how much fuel they used ferrying us about, but we were about to leave the military camp and head into deeper, murkier waters.

Ten minutes later, we'd landed at our next destination, the Navy camp. The military quickly said their goodbyes and off they went. It was a compete mystery quite what was in store for us over the next few hours. Immediately after departing the helicopter, we were greeted by the Navy chief commander, who would be looking after us for the afternoon. The first thing that caught my attention were the huge high-powered boats docked just metres away from where we'd landed.

Although the camp layout looked very similar to the military base, there seemed to be a different feel to this section. Everything felt slightly more relaxed, or at least that's what I thought until the chief commander spotted one of his soldiers walking past who had completely ignored us. He started yelling at him in Spanish. The soldier looked terrified, so much so that I almost stood to attention myself. Seconds later he walked over to us.

'Welcome to the Colombian Navy'.

We were in for an interesting afternoon.

After a quick tour of the camp, Johnny pulled Amber and me to one side to speak about how the day was going to work. Unfortunately for me, Johnny had advised that I would be sitting out on the Navy interviews. It was up to Amber to keep the ship afloat in broadcasting terms while I sat back and watched. At the time I was a little pissed off, but then I remembered two days before that I'd interviewed the speedboat driver on my own in Turbo. Knowing he was on a completely different side of the conflict between the drug lords and the law to the Navy, it made sense. What if I was asked about the man I'd spoken to? I didn't think the change of roles between interviewer and subject would help the programme or me.

Although I wasn't on camera, I could hear every word that was being said between Amber and the chief commander. He even spoke a little English which helped. Johnny had asked Amber to try and find out how they dealt with the so-called 'speedboat drivers' who I had met. But before she had time to even propose that question, we were all asked to jump onboard one of their many vessels. Amber had the choice of which and she picked well, the speedboat!

This speedboat though, was no ordinary speedboat. It was huge, again armoured with guns both to the front and rear. I tried to imagine how a smuggler on a narrow canal boat would feel about fleeing the Navy. With ten or more soldiers joining us onboard, it felt like again we were heading out on a live mission. Still totally unaware of the plan, I took my seat at the back of the boat and just went with it.

Suddenly I heard the commander shout above the buzz of the engine and the froth of waves flying out behind us.

'OK, listen up. Once we leave this base we are in open waters. That means there is a chance we may be called elsewhere to intercept any problems which arise. Hopefully, that will not be the case and we can do a short interview out at sea.'

After repeating it in Spanish, the driver got the go ahead to pull away from the dock. I remember looking back towards the Navy camp in total awe of my surroundings. The huge boats made the buildings look like monopoly houses, with greenery gaping over the waters making it look like a scene out of *Crocodile Dundee*. I just hoped I didn't need so much as a butter knife while I was at sea.

Sitting on a boat which had a full canopy, a steering wheel and ten armoured soldiers certainly felt different to being out alone with a member of the Gulf Cartel. I couldn't have felt in safer hands. As the boat began to speed up, I was almost thrown back into my seat by the power of the engines. With Amber and the rest of our team sitting at the front working on the interview, I almost dozed off to sleep alone at the back.

Suddenly I heard a call over the radio. My immediate thought was that a live mission was about to start again, and I was right. Only this time, we were on our way to intercept 'a large vessel acting suspiciously', as described by the commander. They were just a few minutes away. Instantly I noticed a change in the demeanour of everyone on the boat, including myself. What if it was the man I interviewed? Would he think I'd led the feds to his hull?

The driver had told us to hold tight, so I grabbed onto the handle attached to the side of the speedboat and off we went, skidding across the sea at a stupidly fast speed. I thought in the past I'd been on a fast boat, but that was just a banana boat. This one could really split.

Seconds later we were trailing behind the suspicious looking boat. The earlier panic of possibly bumping into the same smuggler I'd interviewed quickly went overboard, as the boat was huge, much bigger than the one I'd been shown two days earlier. This was more like a large fishing boat. Maybe they were just able to carry more cocaine.

Before I even had time to blink, we were travelling directly side-by-side with the boat in question. Although we were only metres away, I couldn't see a single person on the other boat. Suddenly, the engines cut out and it came to a stop. Something felt strange. All eyes and weapons were directly pointed at the vessel and the commander shouted something in Spanish over to the boat. Instantly four men came from nowhere and appeared on the deck. It almost felt like they had the upper hand - we were on a speedboat with not much protection and they were on a huge wooden boat that towered over us.

Johnny knew this was the right time to start filming. It was perfect footage for the documentary and it almost seemed too good to be true. The Navy quickly jumped onboard the other boat and began to search it, while Amber, Johnny, Oliver and I remained behind with a few protection soldiers.

We all waited nervously across minutes that felt like hours. Finally, the crackly call came through on a radio that the commander had declared the boat to be clear. Part of me was disappointed that nothing had been found. Not for the sake of the documentary, but for the Navy themselves. The readiness in the crew was second-to-none, and their well-executed mission had been timed and performed to perfection, but all for a false alarm. It made me wonder how much of their lives was lived in a state of high alert for a reality that would constantly fall short. Searching a fifty-foot boat in less than ten minutes was an incredible act to carry out, and it must have happened so regularly that everyone slotted straight into their roles, danger or not.

There could have been anything on there. Obviously, drugs being smuggled would be useful to find, as the Navy always wants to pull the narcotics out of circulation. But was it the most worthwhile capture? Information was the currency on those boats, and each side knew it. If a drug dealer was taken and questioned, that was one thing, but a link man? A kingpin? Those types always seemed to elude the authorities, relying on a chain so long that any tug on the end gave them enough of a warning to wriggle off it and start a new one as the most important, yet distant link in that new chain.

None of that made the actions of the Navy themselves any less brave. They were incredibly dedicated and fought a fight they knew could end very badly for them. With dangerous men in the drug smuggling business, knowing that if they get caught, they potentially have a lifetime of regret to look forward to in a cramped jail, the actions of those dangerous men to escape their fate could be anything. A Navy crew member could easily kick open a door and be faced with the business end of a weapon, gun, knife or otherwise.

Amber conducted a short interview with the chief commander at the front of the boat as we cruised back to base. It was full of the positivity and demonstration of power that I'd come to expect from the authorities in Colombia, but as I sat with the rolling waves at my back, I wondered just how much of his bluster was true, and how much was just fascination. It had been an interesting morning, brought to a conclusion when the Navy commander ordered the driver to crank up the speed.

As we rocked and swayed across the open waters, I pictured in my head the speedboat man I'd met two days earlier doing his best to get away. I know which side I'd rather have been on.

Minutes later, we'd reached dry-land.

Our fears about another night of Navy hospitality - and accommodation - were eased when our eighth helicopter ride of the trip took us back to Apartadó. The four of us were getting used to it by now, and back at the police station, we noticed a change in atmosphere. It was busy - a hive of activity with officers chasing up the next lead, the next bad guy, the next potential drop. It could turn out to be nothing, or it could be the vital link that snaps the chain. We didn't get to find out.

Our time with the military and Navy was over.

An hour later we'd arrived back at the hotel, I was shattered - If travel tires the mind, then my body (and seemingly everyone else's) had followed suit. It was only 7pm, but knowing we had to travel back to Medellín when the sun rose, it was time for bed.

Chapter Thirty-Seven

It was time to head back to Medellín. After a long few days in the North of Colombia, I couldn't wait to get back to see the others, find out what they'd been up to and hopefully have a much-needed night out. They had been into the jungle and I was eager to see how their trip had been. Although I'd only known the crew for the best part of a month, I was also looking forward to seeing George, Ivan and our Medellín driver again. It's amazing how quickly working in such intense quarters can bring you close to people you hadn't known just weeks earlier.

Taking the trip to the North had certainly been a huge highlight in the journey and something I would never forget. From sitting inches away from a hitman to landing in Black Hawk helicopters I almost felt like I'd been in one big dream. My initial feelings of having drawn the short straw by going North rather than into the jungle had gone straight out the coach window.

Knowing we had a ten-hour trip back to Medellín certainly *wasn't* one of my highlights, however, and there wasn't much chat between the team on the coach. Everyone was so tired, both physically and mentally. The only conversation which did stick out came courtesy of Johnny.

'When we do arrive back in Medellín, please do not chat to Chanel and Troi about what we have been up to until the cameras are rolling.' They wanted our reactions caught fresh on camera and I understood why - our camaraderie couldn't be faked. Johnny wanted it coming through as pure as Colombian cocaine.

We finally arrived back at the hotel deep into the evening. As I stepped off the coach, I could see Chanel and Troi in their usual positions sitting poised on the hotel balcony. I was desperate to run over and say, 'Wow you'll never guess what we've been up to…', but I knew I had to wait.

After quickly getting changed, the whole team was finally back together and ready to head out to a nearby restaurant. Knowing everyone was safe came as a huge relief.

As we sat down for dinner, it was becoming more and more difficult not to chat about our findings whilst we'd been separated. The crew instantly realised, so delayed eating and decided to set up a scene outside the restaurant to chat about our days away. Obviously, I'd seen and heard about what goes on in the Colombian jungle on YouTube, like many people, but hearing the truth from someone who'd been there in person, someone I knew, would be that much more intriguing.

The scene was set. Amber and I sat on one side of the table whilst Chanel and Troi sat opposite. It almost felt like we were interviewing each other. The cameras started to roll, and Chanel was quick to open the questions; 'So what have you two been up to?'

I was first to respond.

'Wow is all I can say, there's so much we have covered.'

'While you've been out in the Jungle,' Amber chipped in, 'We've been out with the Colombian military, the Navy and we also interviewed a hitman.'

'Serious?' Troi looked stunned. 'What the fuck!'

'Yeah it's been a mad few days,' I continued, 'I even met a smuggler who drives speedboats out of the country. What have you been up to?'

Chanel couldn't wait to tell us.

'Well, we trekked through the jungle in thirty-five-degree heat to visit a man who runs a coca farm. It's crazy how they make it. Oh, and you won't believe it - I met a fucking hit-*woman*!'

After Amber and I had interviewed the hitman, I didn't think anything could top that, but after hearing Chanel had gained access to a hit-woman, I was in disbelief. I wanted to know more but the crew quickly stopped us. They wanted us to just naturally talk about it throughout the rest of our time, either that or they were too hungry to continue!

After that short conversation, we'd finally finished filming for the day. We were free to talk about what we wanted and off camera there was certainly a lot more said. Apparently, the hitwoman who Chanel had interviewed had killed over three hundred people!

I turned to Amber.

'I thought ours was bad for killing five!'

Chanel and Troi then told us over dinner that the gentleman who ran the coca farm had been falsely promised by the government that they would supply him with enough funds to give up growing coca. They said they would help him convert his farm into growing fruit and vegetables. Apparently, they'd promised him that for several years but still nothing had changed.

With four days of heavy filming, I knew this was the night to go out. It was late and the crew were ready to head back to the hotel. I think the fact that they knew we'd been out previously gained us that trust to allow us to stay out for a few extra drinks. So much so that, of course, we ended up in a Colombian club partying until three in the morning.

Chapter Thirty-Eight

It was daylight, and I woke up in a daze. A few drinks, a great night out painting Colombia's heaving tourist trap of Medellín a deep shade of red had been exactly what I needed, just as the eight hours sleep had been too. It was the only time I'd had a full night's sleep in a while. I felt like my batteries had been reset and I was raring to go again. This time, though, I knew my adventure in Colombia was nearly over.

With my head still banging from the alcohol, I was struggling to get up and out of bed. Then suddenly there was a weary knock on the door from Chanel.

'Louuu, we're heading to McDonalds for breakfast - are you coming?' I quickly shot up out of bed and marched downstairs. It was the first time I'd been offered anything to eat for breakfast that I actually wanted, for over a week!

Once I'd arrived at the dining area, I was even more happy to hear that one of the crew had offered to head to McDonalds for us, to save us leaving the hotel. It felt like a day off, nice and chilled, and as I took my usual seat, I spotted Johnny and George going through the footage of the past few days on their laptops. 'Rushes' as they say in the biz. I was buzzing with how it looked. Seeing the country brought to life in the way we'd tackled it fascinated me. If I was watching it on TV, I'd want to keep watching, and that's the best selling point any show can have.

As there was nothing planned for the day, Chanel, Troi, Amber and I found ourselves chatting for over two hours about the past few days we'd experienced. Troi was in complete shock that we'd been on Black Hawk helicopters, whilst I couldn't get over the coca farmer using petrol, battery acid and other disgusting materials to make cocaine.

The day was flying by and we barely moved. It was mid-afternoon when we received a text from the crew. 'Tonight,

Troi and Louis, you will be filming with a tour guide around Medellín square. It will only be something quick, so nothing to worry about. Amber and Chanel, you guys can relax.'

Later that evening, Troi and I were ready for another night filming. Johnny had informed us that we'd be having a stroll around Medellín square asking a tour-guide a few questions about cocaine in the area and life in Colombia in general. Although I'd been in Medellín for some time, there was still a few questions that had gone unanswered.

Once we'd arrived at Medellín square, we met up with a gentleman who had lived in the area for over twenty years. He was very familiar with how the drugs trade worked around Medellín, and he also knew the political side of it. With music blasting from the open doors of nearby clubs and restaurants, Troi and I found ourselves strolling around the square looking like local celebrities. The cameras were bright, and all attention was on us.

I wanted to know a little more about the prices of cocaine for a tourist and a local.

'So, if I was to approach a street dealer now, how much would it cost me for a gram of cocaine?'

'Usually, they don't sell one gram, its either two grams at a time or a little more. As a tourist you would pay around sixty thousand pesos. That's the equivalent of fifteen pounds. I'm guessing that's a lot cheaper than at home.'

'So, if you or another local were to approach them, how much would they charge you?'

'A resident would pay around thirty-thousand pesos. Around seven pounds.'

It made sense that tourists were getting charged more, but I struggled to understand the amounts they were dealing with. Two grams at home on the street would be close to one-hundred and fifty pounds, and close enough to put anyone in a real mess if it was good quality, or it could fuel a heavy addiction if it was pure.

The real business of cocaine was making the drug a turn-off.

Troi wanted to know a little more about life in the area that was vastly populated with tourists, especially the ones who were clearly there for the cocaine.

'You mentioned you have lived over here for twenty years. What is it like living in an area where tourists visit just for drugs?'

'I suppose it brings good and bad to the area', he said. The lights from the camera were brighter than any streetlight as we overtook revellers stumbling up and down kerbs.

'You can say things about many places, like Amsterdam or even Las Vegas - we all know what these areas are known for. It can be looked at both ways.'

I couldn't help noticing how relaxed the so-called tour guide was about the whole cocaine industry. None of the questions we asked seemed to faze him and I got the feeling that he'd heard them a thousand times before.

Filming was over. I'd completely forgotten that it was our final night ahead of our last day in Colombia. That night, no-one was staying out late. It was time to go home.

Chapter Thirty-Nine

It was our final day in Colombia and our time was nearly up. I'd met and seen some incredible people - mostly criminals, but they all had their reasons behind why they do these jobs.

With the flight booked for 9pm we had a full morning of filming pick-ups. These were inserts, missing pieces of information that link up previous content that the producers or directors of any project think you're missing. Sometimes it's purely audio, set over footage of the location but other times, they'd need us in the location itself and we were only in Colombia for a matter of hours.

The rest of the afternoon would be spent packing to go home. Surely there weren't going to be any more surprises?

As much as I wanted to stay in Colombia for a while longer, I'd seen pretty much everything, from the green mountains to the slums. All my thoughts were heading towards touching down in London and eventually arriving back in my hometown of Manchester.

I had little time to think, as minutes later we were on the coach yet again ready to head to another part of Medellín. This time to film our final words.

As the coach pulled up at the top of the glorious mountain, I couldn't help noticing how quiet everyone was, myself included. I think the whole trip had finally settled in. Johnny wanted us to film a brief closing interview, all individually.

I wasn't quite sure why we'd been brought to the top of a mountain, but the views were unreal. I suppose it was a great place to wrap up what was a truly life changing experience. As I stood in front of the camera waiting to be grilled with questions for the final time, I couldn't help but feel slightly emotional.

Johnny broke the silence, as he had so often during the trip.

'So, Louis, what do you think of Colombia?'

I swallowed back the tears.

'I think it's a place like no other. The people here are incredibly strong and caring, not what I expected when the journey started. I said that the country is known for murders, drugs and dirty money. It's a lot more than that.'

'Seeing what you have seen out here, the people you have met. Would that change your opinion on buying the drug again?'

The question was a tough one to answer. I'd completely avoided talking about cocaine personally for over two weeks, so the question stunned me.

'I would certainly think twice about it, knowing that each time I or someone else in the UK does buy the odd gram, that then contributes all the way up to someone being killed for it. It certainly makes you look at it in a different light.'

'Final question, Louis.' Johnny said. 'What would you say to anybody watching the show who maybe wants to buy or try cocaine?'

My answer came immediately and although it was cheesy, it came from the heart. I really meant it.

'I think a lot of drug taking is done on impulse. Just think twice before buying cocaine.'

That was a wrap, for me at least. Amber was next followed by Troi and Chanel. I think judging by everyone's reactions we had all been asked very similar questions, ones which would allow viewers to compare each of our opinions and how they'd changed during the making of the show.

With less than five hours left in Colombia it was time to head back to the hotel, finish our packing and get ready for a long journey home.

Chapter Forty

A fitful final night's sleep, an early wake-up call and no kind of breakfast had meant that my final few hours in Colombia passed in a blur. Before I knew it, I was on a plane out of the country that had changed how I look at the world.

The journey home had felt twice as long as the one out to Colombia, but eleven hours after we set off from Bogota Airport, we touched down in rainy London. It felt as if I'd just come back from travelling for six months, not a fortnight. Despite loving every minute of my time in Colombia, it was so good to be home safe. I couldn't wait to get in my own bed, but I knew that was a long while away.

As I made my way through arrivals with the cast and crew, again I felt slightly emotional. I couldn't believe that I'd just been to Colombia filming a TV documentary. All the things we'd seen came back to me as if on a highlights reel. Medellín Square, the hitman, the speedboat driver, Pablo Escobar's grave, the old lady who couldn't leave her house and, of course, the children. They would grow older now, grow into a life they couldn't control. They stayed with me the most.

Waiting for us in Arrivals was Marc, the series editor.

'Welcome home guys!' he exclaimed, standing there pointing his iPhone at us. The airport wouldn't allow filming, but he wanted to snap our arrival.

'Guys, can you just walk back through the arrivals bit again?'

After an eleven-hour flight it was the last thing any of us needed, more filming! Reluctantly we agreed. I think by this point everyone was overly-tired and slightly moody. With Chanel's Mum waiting in the airport carpark, she quickly made off for Bristol, leaving Troi, Amber and me waiting with the crew for our taxis. I knew I'd be heading back to Manchester in a while. I just didn't know how long.

Half an hour later, I was sat in a black cab in London's busy traffic, raindrops running down the windows, surrounded by grey buildings. It didn't feel real. Just twenty-four hours earlier, I'd been sitting in the sun on the top of a Colombian mountain. I quickly rang my Mum. 'I'm home. Well, I'm just about to jump on the train back to Manchester, so I'll be home in a couple of hours.'

I could hear in her voice she was as buzzing as I was to be home. The train journey back to Manchester flew by. Certain parts of the journey in Colombia kept replaying in my head. The dirt-track road at midnight, banana fields either side of us. Perching on the corner of the speedboat. The coach journeys through winding mountain passes and dew-kissed valleys. I couldn't wait to get home to tell everyone about it, and I didn't really care at that point about the TV side of it, I was just high on the adrenaline of what I'd been through and the fact that my travels were almost over. We all knew that there were follow-ups to be explored once we returned home, but most of the documentary was about what we discovered in Colombia and that voyage of discovery had been the most exciting one of my life.

Five hours after arriving in the capital, I'd reached my hometown. Manchester, city of culture, Northern Soul and barn cakes. Back to where the journey started. From Skype calls to hitman meetings the journey was finally over, for now at least. As I walked through my parents' front door, I was greeted by both my Mum and Dad. The looks on their faces was priceless. It was as if I'd just returned home from a war.

Although I was exhausted, I sat on the sofa for over two hours telling them everything I'd seen and done. They were both shocked. During the little amount of time I'd spoken to them on the phone in Colombia, I only could tell them snippets of what I'd been up to, so it felt great to be able to tell them the full story with no pressure of time. At least, that's what I thought.

A message from Marc flashed up on my phone.

'Hi Louis, hope you got home safe. I'm pleased to say tomorrow you will have the day off. The following day I have booked you a train back up to London. We have several interviews and visits planned. I will send you some more details tomorrow. PS, keep your passport on you.'

I showed my parents the message.

'You best get some rest then, son.'

I finally got into my own bed, and no matter where I've travelled, nothing feels as good as that. It had been something I'd been waiting for since I set off. It must have taken me around thirty seconds before I was out like a light.

The following morning, I woke up feeling disgusting. I must have only had two hours sleep through the night. The jetlag was at its peak. Again, I was unsure of the plan for the week ahead. I knew I'd be heading to London, but for how long? I wasn't sure what else could be covered in the documentary. I'd met pretty much everyone involved in the cocaine chain. Or had I?

At this point, my opinion had changed on cocaine. No longer did I see it as a party drug. I'd seen cocaine in a different light while in its country of origin. If I pay someone for a gram, not only is that money going to the local dealer, it eventually moves up the chain where it is really affecting people, not only in Colombia, but the United Kingdom. I'd seen the drug destroy people's lives and take away their futures. I didn't want to be a link in that chain.

Later that day, I received another message from Marc confirming that the next day I'd be on a train back to the capital. A day of rest and relaxation went by in a flash and before I knew it, I was amid the smoke and traffic of London again, whisked along Euston High Road in a black cab. I hadn't heard from Troi, Chanel or Amber, so when I got to my hotel, I called Chanel.

'Chanel. Hey! I've not spoken to you since we got back. Are you in London?'

She replied; 'No, what are you doing there?'

I was as confused as Chanel. She told me she had a few days off. I found myself in London alone with no clue what was going on. I quickly called Marc who explained I also had the day off, only I was stuck in a hotel away from home. I was apparently on standby in case something popped up. I headed out to grab some food and as I sat down to eat, an even more cryptic message followed. Marc told me that Johnny would be picking me up from the hotel in the morning. I was apparently meeting up with someone who was involved in the dark web.

Now what had I got myself into?

Chapter Forty-One

The only knowledge I had of the dark-web was hearing about it on the news. Apparently, all sorts could be bought on there. I was guessing cocaine was readily available, and that was the reason why I'd be investigating it. I felt slightly nervous again about filming in the U.K. - Colombia had been a wonderful world of different colours, sights and even smells, but being back in the wet streets of London just didn't feel the same.

As I made my way back to the hotel, I started to research the dark web. I was baffled by my findings. You could buy credit card numbers, guns, counterfeit money and even a Netflix lifetime account on there. I then dug a little deeper into the drugs side of it. It appeared as though people from all ages were using it as a supplier... but how? With all websites being untraceable it almost seemed too easy to go on and purchase almost whatever you want. Now, I couldn't wait for the interview.

Just as I arrived back to my room, I picked up a message from Johnny.

'Hi Lou, I will pick you up from your hotel tomorrow at 9am. After the dark-web interview, we have something else planned for the evening, so bring two changes of clothes with you.'

By this point in the journey, I had accepted that I wouldn't be told anything about a new plan until the very last moment. I'd still not heard from Troi or Amber. I was guessing they'd been caught up filming something else, or maybe they were back at home like Chanel leaving me holding the fort.

The following morning, I was in the car on the way to the dark-web interview. Lo and behold I was doing it alone, as only Johnny arrived in the car. Troi was back at home and Amber had been filming something with the National Crime

Agency that morning. The only thing I could focus on was the day ahead.

As we made our way across London to the location, Johnny explained how he wanted the interview to go. The girl we were on our way to meet was a regular buyer of cocaine via the dark web. She was going to show us how it worked. I had so many questions to ask and yet again it was something completely different to the interviews I'd done previously.

When we arrived, I thought we'd stopped off at someone's house. It was, however, the filming location for the afternoon. It was my first time stepping into somebody else's home, interviewing someone on their own soil in England. I felt totally out of my comfort zone. It felt different in Colombia, where everywhere we went was somewhere new and nothing belonged to us. England felt like my country and if every Englishman or woman loved their castle, I was in someone else's.

I wondered if she was buying anything else from the dark web other than cocaine. Johnny knocked on the door and advised me to wait in the car whilst he set up the scene. I was expecting him to get no answer, but she politely opened the door and in Johnny went.

Moments later as I started to nod off, I heard the car door open. It was Johnny.

'Let's go.'

I walked towards the flat and introduced myself to the bubbly young woman at the door. I then stepped inside. I had a stereotypical image in my mind of how someone who used the dark web might look, and she had shattered it with a light smile. I'd wrongly presumed that someone who used it had to be a high-end criminal, or possibly someone involved in organised crime. That didn't seem to be the case. It was someone with a nice flat in central London who seemed to use the dark-web purely to purchase her drugs.

I instantly felt settled. I was ready to go. Well, I thought I was, until I walked into the front room to find she now had a balaclava and sunglasses over her face. I kind of expected she wasn't going to do the interview without covering up, but from a woman who was incredibly bubbly from the minute I walked in, to a woman now masked up felt slightly intimidating.

I took a seat on the sofa next to her. In front of us sat a laptop. After chatting for a few minutes, Johnny started the cameras rolling. It was time for me to be shown what the dark web looked like and how it all worked. I was told by Johnny to prompt her into telling me about the first time she ever used the dark web.

'I started using the dark-web after one of my friends told me about it. They told me it was a lot safer than going out meeting your average street dealer, so I decided to give it a try.'

I was baffled. It almost seemed like an online delivery service, but for drugs. I had to know how it worked and she politely showed me.

'This is what the dark-web looks like,' she said, reaching to the laptop. I couldn't quite believe what I was looking at. It looked very similar to any other major online distributor, except it had pictures of rocks of cocaine with a list of prices next to it. It even had a review section. The woman would check the star rating and then order her chosen piece of cocaine. She showed me that the one she used, had enjoyed a five-star approval.

'This is most likely going to be the best one. There are around five websites you can purchase it from.'

The casual nature of the discussion was something I almost found more disturbing than the brutal reality of cocaine production and export back in Colombia. I couldn't believe that you just typed in a website and a menu of drugs simply popped up ready for checkout. I asked whether I would be able to access the dark web from my own laptop. She told me it wasn't that easy.

'You must have a special software to download it. Once you know how to use it, it's quite simple. I usually use a fake name, so once it is delivered to my home address, if they do find it then I can say it wasn't me.'

I thought the delivery process might be the special, secret part, but I couldn't have been more wrong. She told me that the cocaine would be delivered within a fortnight, and that she'd never been caught buying from the dark web.

'I think it's a lot safer buying it online than going into central London to meet a street dealer who could potentially harm me.' She explained. I was in complete shock how easy it seemed. Johnny quickly paused the interview.

'I think she has a delivery unopened which she would like to show you' said Johnny.

Within seconds the cameras were back rolling. She pulled out a small package from behind the sofa and started to open it. It looked like any normal package you would receive.

'Royal Mail deliver it to my front door,' she told me when I questioned if it was a private courier.

I turned my head slightly and rolled my eyes. The closer she was to opening the package the more excited I was to see what was inside. Seconds later she pulled out a small tube wrapped in paper. She then ripped it open to find a packet of fruit pastilles. At first, I thought she'd been ripped off and they had sent her a packet of sweets, but she explained that it usually arrived exactly the same way.

'Once I open up the packet in the middle there should be cocaine.'

True enough, there it was. A small, white-coloured rock lay inside the packet. Packed around it were actual real Fruit Pastilles. She offered me one and laughed.

'So how much is there?' I asked.

'There's around two grams in there. It's usually a lot better than the stuff on the streets.'

I wasn't sure how much of that I believed. I kept thinking - 'If Amber found Levamisole in her cocaine sample, what on Earth is in that?'

The interview was coming to a close. I'd only been in the flat less than one hour, but I felt I'd learnt a lot. I was confused as to how a woman who seemed to live a normal life in a normal home was using the dark-web. What had led her to that point in her life remained a mystery.

The laptop was then closed, and the interview ended. There was so much more I wanted to ask but time wasn't on our side. I had to quickly get changed in the car outside and head forty minutes across town to pick up Amber.

Johnny and Marc had planned another interview for later in the evening, this time with the owners of a local trap house. At first when I was told, I thought nothing of it. A trap house. It's not meeting a hitman or flying at one hundred and seventy mph in a Black Hawk helicopter across the Colombian jungle. I was in a for a big surprise.

Chapter Forty-Two

It got to around 2pm. We'd picked Amber up successfully and were on route back across London to an unknown location. Knowing the interview with Chanel and the trap house had been cancelled in Colombia, it didn't give Amber and I much hope about this one going ahead. How on earth do you get in touch with an owner of a trap house in the capital city? Never mind someone willing to speak with us on camera.

I had no idea too, until I overheard Johnny on the phone to Marc; 'Amber's now in the car and we're now on our way to meet the fixer. I'll give you a call when I arrive.' It was becoming obvious that these types of documentaries wouldn't go ahead unless a fixer was involved. They seemed to be the most vital person in the show.

Johnny turned to me and Amber after speaking on the phone.

'You probably overheard me talking then, but in case you didn't, we are on our way to meet our local fixer. He will hopefully be taking us to the trap house this evening. With it being a weekend, you can imagine how busy these guys are going to be. Again, there is a chance the interview will be postponed last minute, but just like any other time we just need to be patient and wait for the go-ahead.'

The only time I'd really heard anyone saying 'Trap House' was in a film or earlier in the trip in Colombia. I would have never really thought they existed in the UK but looking back it's kind of obvious. Someone must keep the drugs somewhere. I just couldn't believe people would take the risk of keeping them in central London. The picture in my head I had of a trap house was a rundown building, possibly a high-rise flat away from sight of anybody. You couldn't imagine the police running up fifty flights of stairs without the owner being informed.

I'd heard people back in Manchester selling from one particular house, though I couldn't envision they keep large quantities there. I'm guessing the people who are running these types of houses are quite high up in the chain. It wouldn't be worth owning a trap house for a couple of grams. Surely, we were going to see cocaine in mass quantities!

With all the issues currently surrounding knife crime in the UK, I was probably more nervous about going to meet these guys than I was meeting some of the Colombians. Amber felt the same too. An hour later we'd reached our location. A pub in central London. We were about to meet our local fixer.

As we waited patiently in the car besides a pub, I noticed a young man in his early twenties walking towards us. Johnny turned to Amber and me.

'This is our guy'.

Seconds later the door opened. 'Johnny?', said the fixer. Johnny replied, 'Yeah that's me.' The fixer then took off his baseball cap and jumped in the passenger seat.

Johnny had told us on several occasions that he'd met with everyone we were going to interview prior, but this time it was different. With everyone in the team except Marc heading out to Colombia, the interviews back in the UK were being sourced by him, who as series editor was based in an office in London.

With Johnny clearly knowing just as much as me and Amber, he was quick to speak to the fixer about the scene and how it was going to work. 'I've been in Colombia for the past couple of weeks, so I don't know too much about this. Marc has explained briefly but can you go into the details?'

At first, I wasn't overly pleased going into a potentially dangerous situation with no knowledge of the person we were interviewing. For all I knew, the fixer could have been some random bloke about to do us over. Although he seemed quite calm and relaxed there was still a sense of trepidation.

'Ok, let's move away from here slightly, and then I will explain.' Said the fixer.

A couple of minutes later, the car pulled up in a random street. Everything felt dodgy. The fixer turned to the back of the car and explained how the interview was going to work.

'Obviously, you guys are here to meet with the owners of a trap house. If I told you that you're one hundred percent safe, then I would be lying. With all the street gang violence happening in the UK at the moment, I can't guarantee that.'

He continued; 'Once we're ready to leave, I will ask you to place a blindfold over your head. After that we will drive around for twenty minutes until we arrive at the property. You may think that's slightly strange, but as you can imagine, they do not want the location being known. It's for your protection.'

My heart sunk. I wasn't sure how I felt about being blindfolded and driven to an unknown location by a person I'd never met before. We found out that we would be escorted into the property and once in, we would have an hour to conduct the interview. But, as it was Saturday night, customers would be in and out while the interview would be taking place.

The local fixer advised us that the gang were happy for us to film but they required masks to cover their faces. He then told us there will most likely be four people in the house. Three of them were happy to be filmed, the other would sit out.

The fixer then told us that he would go and visit the property to make sure that all was OK. Apparently, the trap house was only ten minutes around the corner. It felt slightly strange that we were in the middle of London and the den in which they were keeping the cocaine in mass was only minutes away; Amber and I still had no idea where it was.

With the spare time we had while the fixer went to check out the place, we went and grabbed something to eat. Johnny nipped off to the shop whilst Amber and me ate. He came back with three masks, obviously for the people we were interviewing.

It felt slightly weird that I'd only been back in the UK just over forty-eight hours and I was already meeting up with yet another gang. Johnny explained how it was all going to work. 'Once the fixer gives us the all clear he will pick us up. After we get in the car, he will blindfold us. This is quite normal for this type of situation. That's simply if anything does go wrong, we can't be blamed for knowing the location.'

If Johnny was telling us the plan, then that was what we were going to do. We'd gone halfway around the world doing what he had advised us, and we trusted him to take us that step further, especially since we were home. But, like so much I found out making the documentary, I was about to discover that there was nothing scarier than the world you don't see that exists on your doorstep.

Minutes later, the fixer arrived back from the trap house.

'Jump in, we're ready to go!'

I felt more nervous entering this car than I had done when I was sat next to a hitman in Colombia. I think it was the fear of the unknown, driving around totally clueless of our next location. Although the fixer was on our side, I just didn't feel comfortable putting a blindfold over my face for twenty minutes whilst we drove around central London. To be killed in Colombia would have been awful yet seen as part of the risk of travelling to a dangerous country looking for drug-related drama. Getting killed on the streets of my own country's capital suddenly scared me more. It all seemed a little too much, too real. Surely what we were doing would attract some sort of unwanted attention.

As I took a seat in the back of the car next to Amber and Johnny, the fixer turned his head towards us and politely asked us to place the black blindfolds over our heads. He then asked us to crouch down as much as possible to avoid anyone seeing us. I couldn't see a thing. As the car pulled away from the pavement my mind was playing tricks on me. I felt anxious, the hairs on my arm standing on end and my neck feeling hot. Having a blindfold over my face certainly didn't help me relax.

The car was silent. After ten minutes driving around, I'd had enough. I've never been a fan of being bossed around so I instantly thought to myself; 'What's the worst that can happen if I take it off?' Then I realised the actual situation. I was no longer at school or work where the worst thing could be a telling off. I could have put myself or everyone else's life in danger, so I decided to leave it on.

Twenty minutes felt like a lifetime and the car finally came to a halt. We had to assume that we'd arrived at the trap house. I had no idea what was coming next. Surely, the fixer wasn't going to ask us to leave the car with our blindfolds still on?

Sure enough, he did.

The three of us were individually escorted into the trap house still fully blindfolded one by one. As I stepped out of the car and was physically guided by the fixer, I tried to imagine what it looked like for any neighbour peeking out of the window. I must have looked like a hostage. Then I realised, crime on that sort of level would surely mean anyone in the area would be paid not to say a word.

With my head pointed down towards the ground and back bent, it felt very similar to when I was out with the military on the battlefield, only this time I was in central London about to interview a load of drug dealers. Johnny was first in, followed by me and then Amber. I couldn't wait to take off the blindfold to see what the place looked like, but before that we were advised to wait until all doors were closed by the fixer.

We got the all clear.

As I slowly removed my blindfold, three males stood right in front of me. All of them were six foot plus. Slightly dazed from the light, I didn't have a clue what to say. I turned to Johnny to the right of me to break the ice. Again, he did so; 'Hi guys, thank you for inviting us here. I'm not quite sure where you want to conduct the interview?'

I couldn't believe how chilled out they were. All of them had a welcoming feel to their drug den. I was expecting to walk in and be pinned to the wall and searched. That wasn't the case and they seemed to relish our visit.

'Come on in, we will do it in the lounge area. We need to make sure that none of the house is filmed which will be recognisable.'

With the fixer being the go between, he pulled Amber and myself to the side whilst Johnny went into the living room.

'I'm sure you're used to this advice now, but if the dealers aren't willing to answer a question then please move on.'

Seconds later, the one thing I really wanted to avoid happened. I needed the toilet. As I walked into the living room to find Johnny setting up the scene, I felt like a little boy at school. I wanted to ask them to use their bathroom, but I wasn't overly confident walking around the house alone knowing I could be blamed at any moment for some of their drugs going missing. But I had to ask. I had to go.

'Can I use your toilet?'

The response I got from one of them was - 'Of course mate, upstairs, turn right and you'll see it.'

I was worried I'd need escorting, but I made the brave decision to leave the living room alone and head upstairs. Walking around a trap house was a very weird feeling. Every single window from top to bottom was covered with either a curtain or some sort of newspaper. I couldn't understand how from the outside it didn't look slightly strange. Although the interview hadn't started, looking around the house it was obvious from the lack of decor that it wasn't a place in which they were living. There was hardly any furniture and the walls were bare. Everything was non-descript, as if it could be anywhere, a home with no distinguishing features, apart from the sellotaped sports section of the Daily Star blocking the view from the bathroom window.

As I stood over the toilet waiting on a nervous wee, I heard something right behind me. I didn't dare look round. I had a feeling it was someone watching over me and I was right. As I left the toilet, I looked left to find a young lad, only in his twenties just standing there on the veranda. I didn't know what to say so I decided to nod and avoid asking what he'd been doing watching me. The nod, the all-male gesture that escapes a thousand awkward situations. An embarrassing queue for a gap at a packed urinal in a football stadium. That moment ordering a drink at a bar just before the guy who knows it's your turn. Or a young man watching you piss in a top-secret drug trap house. Classic nodding territory.

I almost knew the reason behind it so there was no thought in the back of my head something dodgy was going on. As I walked back into the lounge area Johnny had already set up the cameras and was ready to go. I'd still hardly made any contact with any of the dealers, so I wanted to gain a bit of rapport.

'Is the guy upstairs not joining in on the interview?'

They replied through giggles.

'No, he's a little camera shy.'

Shortly after a quick discussion between the lot of us, it was decided that we would interview just one of the men whilst the other two would sit and watch. At first, they were super paranoid about the cameras catching any of the house which would give it away, so Johnny had made the decision that one of the dealers could check out the angles before we started.

After putting up several bedsheets on the wall to avoid showing any sort of wallpaper, the interview was ready to go. Amber and I sat on one side of the dining table and our interviewee sat on the other. On went the mask to cover his face and the questions started.

'Can you tell me what happens in a typical trap house?' I asked.

'This is the place we keep and distribute our food.'

Food?

'I guess that means drugs?'

'Yeah, mostly cocaine, but other drugs too,' he said, not in the slightest bit ashamed of it being illegal, albeit a little hesitant. Since the cameras had started to roll, the persona of the dealers seemed to change. Although we knew they meant business, it almost felt like they'd suddenly realized the situation they had put themselves in. We still wanted to understand the process in a little more depth.

'People come here to collect their food,' he went on. 'We have a few dens. In this particular one, due to the location, we have to be quite careful.'

Amber was quick to ask how much cocaine was stored in the house.

'Around fifteen ounces of cocaine are kept here,' he replied.

I was in total disbelief. How was a house in central London being used to hold a street value of twenty-thousand pounds worth of cocaine and getting away with it?

'Surely you don't live here?' I asked.

'No, I don't. We always have someone in the house though, just in case anybody tries anything. I live quite far away.'

Although this gang was clearly making huge profits, none of them seemed to be very flash with the cash. The house was run down and none of them had particularly stunning watches or jewellery. I wanted to question that.

'Obviously, you're making massive amounts of money off this, or surely you wouldn't be risking your lives to do it. What's the reason behind it?'

'It's not really about the money for me. I get a buzz off giving people a good time. Whereas other dealers are there just for the money, I make sure all my customers are happy. That way they stay loyal to me' he said, to my obviously shocked face. 'I have made many friends doing this.'

I wanted to know how a typical buyer would go about contacting him and visiting the trap house, if they did at all, but he answered with a laugh.

'If you don't know my number, or know me in person, there is no way you are visiting this den. I only allow loyal customers here. If a new customer does come along, they will be met elsewhere by the guys on the ground.'

The guys on the ground?

'Yeah, the youths I have working for me. Street-dealers.'

As if by coincidence, there was a knock at the door. I immediately panicked. I looked to Amber next to me and she looked like she'd just seen a ghost. It was all over for us if the police were knocking.

'Don't worry. We're expecting someone. Please turn off the camera's and put them away, just in case', said the dealer stood behind Johnny. Johnny did what was asked of him and all three of the dealers left the lounge area and walked towards the front door all in sight of us. Waiting for that door to be unlocked and opened, I felt like I was about to find out the contents of my box on Deal or No Deal.

The door swung open and there stood a lad in his late teens. The owners of the trap house were obviously aware of his face because they quickly invited him in. There were now five people, plus us in the house. We were outnumbered.

'Is this guy part of your crew?' asked Johnny, looking slightly worried. More laughter.

'No, he's a customer. You guys can film him collecting some food if you want.'

Johnny was happy to, and the customer was given a mask to shield his identity. He was filmed 'arriving' in the living room and paying for his cocaine.

'How much is he buying here?' we asked, and the dealer told us.

'He is picking up one ounce. That should last him for the weekend.'

'The weekend?! Twenty-eight grams will be sold over the weekend just by him?'

'Yeah, that's minor work.'

As a person who has openly admitted buying drugs in the past, I knew how awkward it could be sometimes, picking them up. No-one enjoys the transaction, but both sides almost always end up happy with the deal. It's an odd situation but walking into a trap house whilst a documentary is being filmed is something neither I nor any of my mates had come across. The customer was told to keep the pick-up quiet and off he went.

The interview had certainly revealed some interesting things, but there was one final question I wanted to ask, and I didn't want him, or the other two dealers standing at the side of Johnny to get the wrong end of the stick.

'You and your colleagues are distributing cocaine in huge quantities. How far up the chain would you guys say you are?'

'We are near the bottom, trust me. The people you have met in Colombia are the top of the chain. The people who distribute it in the UK are only guinea pigs for the cartels at the top, the ones who are shipping tonnes over each year.'

It all made sense. If the guys in that house had any power, it was only over those they chose to sell their stuff to, an ounce at a time. The people with real power were the distributors back in Colombia, who were shipping it out in massive quantities. They cut it, they led the pricing for it and they essentially controlled the market, supply and demand. As dangerous as it all was, the same principles applied to a paper-shop supplying copies of the Daily Mail to their customers.

As the interview had finished, we were escorted out of the back of the property and into the car. We left as quietly and as anonymously as we had arrived, and both Amber and I sat in a stunned silence for a while. We'd had a seat in what felt like another world, an underworld that most normal people don't ever get to see. What shocked me most was how visible the house must have been. The papered-over windows, the lack of any decoration inside; they couldn't have looked more conspicuous if they'd tried. But they were hidden in plain sight, and that was their trick. It was like chewing gum in class at school; do it sneakily and they spot you every time. Do it openly as if you're taking the piss and no-one is ever any the wiser.

Dropped back at the pub, we were filmed and asked about the interview by Johnny. Luckily it was short n sweet and after another crazy day, I was relieved to be getting on a train home from London to Manchester. The plan was to have one rest day, then head back up to London for some final interviews. Although the adventure had been the best thing that I'd ever taken part in, I just couldn't wait to get home.

Crammed in among dozens of commuters who were making their regular trip North to their homes, I was trying my best to guess what they did for a living. Maybe they'd been in the office, maybe out and about in London. There could be a busker, a banker and a businessman all sitting on the same table as me. But I'd spent the day talking about the dark web and being driven blindfolded to a trap house, and not one of them would have ever guessed.

What a strange feeling that was.

Chapter Forty-Three

I kept replaying everything in my head. The key moments of the journey. Most of them were positive ones but others made me slightly sad. I was worried that maybe along the way I had said something stupid on camera which I would later regret. I just think that comes naturally when you've been under intense pressure for such a long amount of time. You're not in post-production, you don't get to tweak your angles, pick the shots that make you look good. It's all sacrificed for the story, and that's absolutely the way it should be, too. The end is always more important than any one part of the puzzle.

Four hours later, I was back home. Greeted again by my parents, they couldn't wait to hear what I and the rest of the crew had been up to. Now wasn't the time, I said. I was far too tired. I casually walked up the stairs, lay on my bed and within seconds I was out like a light.

The following morning, I was up before sunrise. Totally unaware of the days ahead, I quickly packed a small suitcase, said my goodbyes to my parents again and headed back to London.

The minute I arrived at Euston station, I received a text message from the crew.

'Lou, where are you?' We're waiting in a car outside the station.'

At the time, I was in no mood to rush, but I knew we had to be somewhere by a certain time. I just didn't know where. I'd finally found the car which was waiting for me. In the car were Chanel, Troi, Amber and Johnny. There was one person missing.

'Where's George?' I asked.

Johnny replied; 'He is in Weston Super Mare at the moment. That's where we're heading right now.'

'What are we going there for?' I replied.

Before Johnny even had time to respond, Troi shouted; 'We're heading to a rehab centre.'

'Thanks for that Troi' said Johnny. 'Yes, we are visiting a rehab centre. This is something totally different to anything we have done on the series, so it should be great. There may be people there who may be incredibly sensitive, so we have to be very careful what questions we ask.'

Twenty minutes before, I was on a train listening to Bob Marley singing 'Don't Worry, Be Happy.' Now I was feeling like I should have skipped to Amy Winehouse wailing 'No, no, no,' to rehab. I was quite shocked to say the least. With a three-hour journey to north Somerset on the horizon, there was plenty of time to think.

Checking in to a rehab centre is something I'd never really wanted to do, but under the circumstances, and after my initial listlessness had worn off, I couldn't wait to get there. I'd always been interested in knowing how the process works, from beginning to end. I was intrigued to find out what life is like to live there as an addict. I'm sure working there would also be no easy task, either.

We were about to get the opportunity to meet and speak with some of the people who had been affected by cocaine and possibly other addictions. At the start of the process, I was totally clueless about cocaine being addictive. Clearly, I'd been blind to it. Maybe I'd always seen it as the drug you take occasionally. I'd seen signs of it, but I'd just never put it all together. It hadn't added up until I'd seen exactly from where it came. Colombia.

Halfway through the trip, Johnny swivelled his head towards the back of the car.

'Once we arrive at the rehab centre, the management in charge will explain the day in detail. You are most likely going to be split into pairs. Throughout the day, we expect you to be sitting in on meetings, open discussions and such. Some of you may be asked to speak individually to people.

There will be a gentleman who is coming in later in the afternoon who has successfully completed rehab. He will be chatting with one of you individually.'

The day ahead sounded extremely engaging and one hour later we'd arrived in Weston Super Mare. I had a picture in my head of what a typical rehab centre would look like, but I'd got it completely wrong. The place we'd turned up at looked more like a huge mansion. A place that, from how it looked on the outside, I certainly wouldn't mind living in. As I stepped out of the car onto a bright pebbled driveway, I couldn't help noticing a sign hanging in the gardening area. – 'Dream what you want to dream, go where you want to go, be what you want to be.' They were words which stuck in my head from the minute I entered the grounds to the minute I left.

With Johnny and George following our every move on the cameras, it was left to Amber, Troi, Chanel and me to knock on the door. Almost as if it was planned, a woman answered. 'Welcome, come on in.'

As I stepped into the huge hallway, everything around me seemed to be unadorned, like the trap house, except everything was a brilliant white, uninterrupted by bedsheets or wallpaper but decorated with informative or inspiring posters on almost every wall. It was a completely different look to the outside. It felt very school like with a reception area and even an assembly hall. The woman who had greeted us at the door was a matriarchal headmistress-type, probably what was needed in a place like rehab.

Our main aim for the day was to find out about the addictive side of cocaine, and we certainly didn't waste any time in doing so. After being given a quick tour of the centre, we were all gathered outside the assembly hall waiting to sit in on a group meeting along with the current addicts. I'm not a huge fan of using the term 'addicts', but that was part of the battle. Admittance of being an addict was part of the cure. Every journey starts with a single step, I thought.

Before entering the assembly hall, we were told what a typical day would be like for a resident of the rehab centre. I was astounded by the routine which was set out by the staff. From 6.45am when the morning bell goes off, right the way through to 7.30pm was constant work. Some of the things in the schedule were things I'd never even imagined going on at a rehab centre - Tai chi, quigong, relaxation classes, auricular acupuncture and many more. I'd always imagined it to be a very lonely place, somewhere you're constantly looking at your watch. That wasn't the case and it seemed it was working for them after they showed us the success rates.

There must have been twenty plus people already seated waiting for the morning lecture to start. Obviously, they were aware of our arrival, but all eyes turned from the front of the room directly to the four of us. I had to break the silence.

'Hi, do you mind if the four of us sit in on the meeting?'

Almost simultaneously the group said, 'No problem.' Apparently twenty-five percent of them didn't want to be filmed, which was understandable, so they all wore white labels to make sure Johnny or George didn't mistakenly start filming them. I quickly took a spare seat near the front of the class. I managed to get talking with one of the addicts whilst everyone else began to mingle. He was only young, no older than thirty. Without being too pushy, I wanted to know the reasons he was there - was it for alcohol abuse, or even cocaine addiction?

He seemed quite happy to talk, and as if by coincidence he revealed his addiction; 'I kind of know what you want to ask, so I'll just tell you. I'm quite open and honest about it now. I am in here for cocaine abuse.'

Part of me wanted to tap him on the shoulder and say, 'Everything will be good in the end'. But I knew that was the wrong way to go about things. He, like everyone else, was there for a reason, and that reason wasn't to be mollycoddled. It was to quit, once and for all.

The lecture began, firstly with an open discussion about how each of them was feeling at that very moment, there and then. The lecturer said, 'Morning! How is everyone today?' It reminded me of my first day back in school when all the students were gathered in the assembly hall waiting for their forms to be given out. This though, was something completely different. With an average age of around thirty in the rehab centre, everyone seemed very mature.

Many responded. 'Great, fantastic, ready for the day ahead', but others weren't quite as enthusiastic.

Although we had only been in the room for less than five minutes, I couldn't help noticing the passion and power of the female lecturer. Everything she said from the second we walked in felt so believable, so much so that I thought I was in rehab myself. Everyone seemed to be so engaged with what was being said, from the front to the back of the hall.

Our main aim was to talk with people who had a cocaine addiction, but it wasn't that simple. Everyone around us was being treated for different problems, from sex addictions, right the way through to gaming addictions. I thought they would have all been treated in a different way, but after sitting in on the meeting and the lecturer explaining the twelve steps to recovery, I understood why that wasn't the case.

The twelve steps started with honesty and that was followed by hope, faith, courage, integrity, willingness, humility, discipline, forgiveness, acceptance, awareness and finally gratitude. All steps, which, if followed correctly would apparently solve a lot of their problems. Those twelve words certainly got the group thinking.

Each person who stepped into the rehab centre had very different stories to tell, but it was almost impossible to speak to all of them individually. It was time for a quick break, and although I don't smoke, I found myself chatting in the smoking shelter to a lad from the Netherlands. He chose to come to the UK to try and stop his alcohol addiction. He told me that it was 'the best rehab centre in the world.' He also believed taking himself away from everything and everyone was the way to solve the problem. So much so, he left his own country.

Without the cameras rolling, I knew I could ask any question I wanted.

'What is it actually like living here?'

'To be honest,' he replied, whilst looking over his shoulder, 'it's not that bad, but don't tell the staff that. It's better than my usual daily routine.'

'And that is?' I asked.

'I would usually wake up around 8am, go to the shop to buy a bottle of vodka and then drink until I pass out.'

It sounded like a vicious circle of sleep, eat, drink, repeat, just probably without the eating. It certainly didn't sound healthy and he was definitely in the right place for help. Step 1 of honesty had been taken care of, but I figured hope might be harder to nail down.

'Louis!' Johnny shouted at me as we returned to the room.

'Yeah, what's up?'

'Have you brought your passport?'

'Yeah, Marc told me to keep it with me, why?'

'Don't look too worried. I know it's late, but this afternoon you and I will be heading to Amsterdam for a day. It's a surprise though, so I can't tell you what we're doing.'

Although the rehab centre wasn't over, I already had something else planned. I didn't think that Troi, Chanel and Amber knew about it until they all came outside shouting.

'We know what you're doing in Amsterdam.' At the time, I was a little annoyed, so much so that I was going to refuse to go until I found out. But as the day continued, it was put to the back of my mind. One of us was about to interview a reformed addict who had specifically come back to the rehab centre to meet with us. Who was going to be the one doing the interview?

George quickly made the decision.

'Louis, with you leaving early this afternoon, it would be good to get you interviewing someone earlier. Will you do this one?'

Although I had Amsterdam on my mind, I had to remain focused and ready for the next scene. I followed George into the main reception area and minutes later a gentleman walked through the front doors. All the staff suddenly walked over to him, kissing and cuddling him.

'Welcome back, so good to see you', they cooed.

The lady who initially welcomed us into the centre introduced us to our interviewee, Tony. He seemed very confident and happy to talk with us on camera. I'd usually stereotype a so-called addict as someone who looks a bit frail, a bit scruffy looking, but this man couldn't have looked any different. Dressed smartly from head to toe, I thought at first that we'd got the wrong guy.

With time no longer on our side, the interview had to be quick but detailed. We used a little side room directly opposite the assembly hall. As Johnny had set up the cameras and lighting, we were ready to go. I sat one side of a table, whilst Tony sat on the other.

I'd interviewed a Major general of the Colombian military, a hitman and even a smuggler, but this was something totally different. We were getting into the devastating effects of cocaine, seeing real life problems rather than just the criminal side. Now we were questioning a man who had a rehabilitated success story; something totally new to me. I was nervous.

'Morning Tony. Thank you for speaking with me today. I know it's probably a hard subject to talk about, so just stop me if you no longer want to continue.'

'I'm quite happy to talk about anything really, obviously within reason. I want to use this interview to make people aware of cocaine addiction and say that it is possible to turn your life around. I've finally got my life and family back. It's been over two years clean now.'

I wanted to understand how and when you know that you're a cocaine addict. When addicts realise they need help is often pivotal to their chances of using it.

'Believe it or not, it all started out having a few lines here and there on a night out. Then suddenly it escalated to taking it almost every weekend. After that it got very bad. I was taking it in work, at home, when I woke up. I knew I had a problem when my wife and kids left me.'

'You had a wife and kids at home?'

'Yes! I was that dependent on it. I lost everything, even my job.' He replied.

'Wow!' I said, stunned.

The interview had suddenly turned quite intense. Although I'd only known him for a matter of minutes, I was so glad to see that he had turned his life around. I wanted to know how bad it got, how much he was taking, and just as importantly, how much that cost him.

'One night, I went through fifteen grams. On an average night, it was four to five. I had fifteen-thousand pounds that all went on cocaine. I had to ask my parents for money in the end.'

The light in the room cast him in a kind of halo, nice timing as he spoke about his salvation.

'Checking in to this rehab centre was the best thing that ever happened to me. They changed my life around and I want to thank them for that.'

I found out that the man had put his whole life back together. He'd saved his marriage, and even got his old job back. Everyone around him had been incredibly supportive, and he now lived with his family and worked a decent job. How many people would risk all that by taking drugs? It seemed like this guy would never take it for granted again.

Once again, it had been a whirlwind of a time in the documentary, this time at the rehab centre. I was whisked away, and onto another plane. This time I was heading to one of the drug capitals of the world, for use, trafficking and, perhaps above all in the public consciousness, availability. A city of access to drugs that rivals any across the globe. A neon paradise for some, a drug-filled danger for others, I was about to find out why Amsterdam had a vibe all of its own.

Chapter Forty-Four

Around one hour later, I'd arrived in Amsterdam with Johnny. Although Johnny turned in to a great friend over the journey, it felt slightly unnerving travelling to a different country alone with a television director. When I'd visited Amsterdam previously, it would usually be for a nice chilled weekend with the lads, but I was still totally unaware of my reason for being there. I was starting to worry. I'd already asked Johnny and the crew several times; 'What am I going to be doing in Amsterdam?', but I'd always get the same answer; 'Just wait and see!'

I mean, I like surprises, but turning up in a foreign country not knowing the reason behind it, felt slightly weird. As we headed into the city centre via taxi, I kept trying to think of things that would be associated with cocaine and Amsterdam. I was baffled. All I could think of was the amount of shipments in and out of there, or that it was something to do with smuggling again?

After spending the day at the rehab centre and flying to Amsterdam, Johnny and I were shattered. As we made our way to our rooms Johnny said, 'I'll see you in the morning downstairs around eight.' Although I wanted to almost detour back out of the hotel and into a bar, I knew I'd regret it the following morning.

As I laid down in bed, the day's earlier events were playing on my mind, the rehab centre sticking out the most. I could never imagine myself getting to a stage where I would have to visit somewhere due to an addiction. But as many of them said, it could happen to anyone. I totally believed that was true, and I also knew cocaine was no longer just a party drug.

Cocaine was an addictive drug, and it was so much more. It was an industry, but rather than being full of employees, it was littered with victims, from the children in Colombia who endured hardship and family strife, to the men who transported the drugs cross-country, risking their lives for personal gain. It was hard to think of a link in the chain who wasn't, in some way, a victim, unable to live a life of freedom.

The following morning, I woke up feeling fresh. Johnny and I were up and out of the hotel by 7am. Being in Amsterdam had certainly lifted my mood, but after eating breakfast, that quickly changed. Johnny had revealed the real reason we were in the city of canals and bicycles. We were about to meet a doctor, and not just any old doctor, but a nose specialist.

At first, I was totally confused, I tried to understand how that had anything to do with cocaine. Then I clocked on.

'Before you say anything, it's not as bad as it sounds', said Johnny.

'Wait, so you have brought me to Amsterdam to visit a doctor. What relevance does that have to me?'

I was fuming. I thought I'd be meeting up with the Amsterdam equivalent of Pablo Escobar, not attending an appointment at the doctors. It also didn't help the fact I'd been told it was a surprise. With the whole crew knowing I was very cautious about my perception on camera, I thought they'd chosen the wrong person to visit Amsterdam.

'You have the wrong end of the stick Louis. It's not just like any doctors back home, we are here to discover the affect cocaine has on the nose. That's the nose in general, not yours in particular.'

As we made our way across a busy Amsterdam centre, bicycles zig-zagging across our path through the city, I dropped back, walking alone among the tulips and walkways. It reminded me of falling out with one of my friends on the way home from school when I was a kid. One argument and you'd suddenly end up in a walking standoff. I had no questions for Johnny. I just wanted to get the scene done and fly back home.

Just ten minutes later, we'd arrived at the location, or rather eleven minutes for me, walking as I was a few paces behind Johnny. The place we had just arrived at certainly didn't look like a typical doctor's surgery. Three stories high, it looked more like an expensive London pad in leafy Kensington. If you have ever been to the centre of Amsterdam, through the back alleys and into the quieter parts, you will know exactly what I mean. All the houses look almost identical.

Johnny rung the bell and almost instantly, a lady answered the door with a bright smile on her face.

'Hi, please come in. Follow me upstairs.'

The doctor's surgery I'd just walked in to was fit for a king. The place was like a palace and it was clearly where a lot of rich people went. As I tip-toed upstairs in my trainers, I kept looking behind to make sure I hadn't left any dirt on the carpet, which you could easily lose a shoe in as you walked, it was that thick.

Waiting in the main lounge area was Dr Callum. He greeted us with a kind gentle handshake. We both smiled and returned greetings in kind, and Johnny began setting up the cameras for filming.

I had a little time to speak with Dr Callum off camera, and as we got talking, I think he was as shocked as I had been after finding out I didn't know the reason I was there until minutes earlier. The good doctor tried to put me at ease.

'Don't worry, if you are unhappy with anything then we will stop. To be honest, there is nothing we are going to talk about that is personal to you. I do have a machine I would like to show you later on, but that's entirely up to yourself whether you would like to use it.'

That sounded cool. A machine. What kind of weird contraption...wait, 'use it', as in a machine was going to be used *on me?*

I was confused. I glanced around the room, half expecting to catch a glimpse of the laser beam table that James Bond was strapped to in *Goldfinger*.

Johnny was ready for the interview to begin.

'Let's just quickly run through how this is going to work. Firstly Louis, Dr Callum will ask you a few questions about your past experiences using cocaine, then after that we can go into a little more detail about problems cocaine can cause on the nose.'

I instantly stopped him.

'Wait a second, Johnny. I have come on the show to discover about cocaine. I am not being lectured on camera about my past usage. Do you realise the effects that could have on me and my life?'

We'd hit a real stumbling block for the first time in the documentary.

'You don't even know what he is going to ask you yet.'

I knew I had to stick to my word. There was no way I was being persuaded or pushed in to saying or doing anything I didn't feel comfortable with, so the question was scrapped, and we quickly moved on.

Although Dr Callum was totally on my side, I knew he was also there to do a job. Johnny told me that the team were going to film me listening to Dr Callum. He was going to explain how cocaine can affect the nose. After that he would show me a few images. They might be quite shocking to look at, but as Johnny told me, 'Trust me, it will probably put you off for life.'

He wasn't wrong. It was hard to imagine anyone getting to the stage that one famous actress did, in taking so much cocaine that her septum gave way entirely. We sat around a giant marble table, and Dr Callum showed us images of other noses, ones that had managed to be fixed. Dr Callum wasn't just a resident doctor. He travelled all over Europe fixing the afflicted, a modern-day nose-doctor extraordinaire. He even showed me a fake nose, one that he might have magnetically affixed to a badly affected face.

Finally, Dr Callum showed me 'the' machine in an adjacent room. In it, there was a tiny camera which could be inserted into the nostril to read if the nose had any scarring from past cocaine use. Johnny wanted me to try it out, so I went along with it, though, making it very clear that I was not OK with the footage being used in the documentary.

The interview was over, and Johnny wasn't overly pleased with my refusal to film the results of the scanning machine. We left the doctors and talked it out over a cold beer in an Amsterdam bar. We agreed that I probably was the wrong person to visit the doctor, and I apologised to Johnny for being such a pain. He understood my concerns and by the time our flight came around, we boarded a flight home as friends again.

Johnny dropped me off at Marco Pierre White's hotel in Central London. After a whirlwind twenty-four hours, it was just nice to be back in England, and this time for good.

Chapter Forty-Five

Waking up in a five-star hotel in central London was certainly something I could get used to. I couldn't wait to head downstairs to try their full English, a breakfast I was looking forward to more than the ones we'd been offered in Colombia. As I sat down for my Michelin-starred breakfast, I heard a beep outside the hotel. My phone then started to vibrate. It was Johnny.

'I'm outside. Where are you?'

I was still half asleep and half-empty. I could smell sausages being cooked.

'Hurry up, we are already ten minutes late.'

The whole Amsterdam trip had been one big whirlwind, and I'd completely forgotten that I had yet another long day ahead filming. I quickly ran upstairs, packed my belongings into my case and checked out of the hotel without getting anywhere near so much as a slice of toast, let alone the full English breakfast I'd been dreaming of eating.

As we dashed across London to meet Chanel at the train station, Johnny revealed the plan for the day.

'I've already briefed Chanel. Today we will be heading to Essex. We will be meeting up with a lady who unfortunately lost her son in a car accident. As you can imagine, the subject is going to be incredibly sensitive.'

Twenty minutes later, Chanel was in the car and we were on route to Essex. Seeing her instantly changed my mood from low to high, and although the interview coming up was going to be very difficult, I knew having Chanel there would make it that much easier. Once we were on our way, and with my stomach rumbling, Johnny told us a bit more about why we were about to speak to the lady in question.

'The lady who we are meeting lost her son in a fatal car accident. He was in the pub with his friend totally clueless that he was on cocaine. After getting in the car with him and driving home, they unfortunately hit a roundabout at a high speed.'

When I was first asked to do the show, I knew I'd signed up for meeting with gangsters and addicts. I didn't realise I would now be about to interview someone who had lost a loved one due to the very problem we were exploring. We'd reached the point of meeting one of the many victims of cocaine at the end of the drug's journey - consumption and consequences.

'Once we arrive, the lady we are meeting will get in the car. She has agreed to show us the roundabout where she lost her son. We'll then head back to her home and do a quick interview there.'

Minutes later, we'd picked our interviewee up and were on route to the roundabout. With Chanel seated next to me I knew there would be no chance of any awkward silence. She quickly managed the situation.

'Hi, I'm Chanel, how are you?'

The lady replied, looking nervous.

'I'm good thank you, I love your tattoos!'

Many questions were rushing through my head whilst Chanel was chatting. A lot of them I wouldn't dare ask, but as we pulled up on the lay-by, I had no time to think. Johnny turned his head to the back of the car; 'I think we are here. Are you guys OK?'

Chanel and I didn't speak. The lady did.

'Yeah I'm all good, follow me.'

As we stepped out of the car onto the busy dual carriageway, I couldn't help noticing how fast the vehicles were approaching the roundabout where the fatality happened. Johnny quickly pulled out the camera from the boot of the car and began recording us. Chanel and I stood side by side with the lady as we walked slowly towards the roundabout. I couldn't imagine how she was feeling.

Although she had lost her son where we stood, she seemed so strong and managed to remain calm despite constant beeps coming from cars that passed. It felt like a slight lack of respect, though none of the drivers could have presumed the private horror that the lady at the side of the road was feeling. It was clear from the way she held herself that she had been there before.

Chanel broke the ice.

'So, this is where it happened?'

She replied; 'Yes, this very roundabout. I get shivers down my back every time I visit.

I was a little speechless. I tried putting myself in her shoes, but I just couldn't. Losing a relative is so tough to take, but in the manner that this tragedy happened, I couldn't help thinking that it could have been avoided.

Without being too pushy, I wanted to know more about the circumstances.

'It was late September, a beautiful night. I'd got in to bed around 11pm and nodded off. The next thing, I heard a knock on the door. I immediately panicked and ran downstairs. It was the police.

Chanel and I nodded our heads in acknowledgment.

'They told me that my son had been involved in a very serious car accident. I instantly broke down, falling to the ground. I wanted to think it was all a horrible nightmare. Then my younger son came running down the stairs. That was the moment I knew my life had changed.'

Filming was no longer my main prerogative. Making sure the lady was OK was all that mattered.

'I'm fine. Can we leave here now and head back?'

Instantly, concerned for the welfare of our interviewee, we made our way back to her Essex home and continued the conversation there. This time though, we wanted to know how cocaine had played a part.

Whilst sipping on a cup of tea, relaxed on the sofa, she began to open up a little.

'He'd finished work on a Friday afternoon and came home to get changed. His best friend then called him, asking him to join him in the local pub. As lads do, he went, enjoying the night. Around 11:30pm, they both left the pub and got in the car. His friend was driving while my son was in the passenger seat. Apparently, they hit the roundabout around eighty mph.'

Suddenly a young lad walked in to the living room where we were conducting the interview. He must have only been fourteen years old.

'This is my younger son, my life. I don't know what I'd do without him.'

I struggled to imagine what life was like for the younger son. He'd not only lost his older brother in an unimaginable way, but he now had to be the man of the house and look out for his mother.

Johnny stopped the interview.

'Shall we have a quick break, guys?'

I looked to Johnny; 'I think that's best.'

While the interview came to a halt, Johnny wanted to nip outside to the car. It was chance to get some fresh air, so I joined him, leaving Chanel and our interviewee inside having a cigarette.

'This woman is so brave. I can't believe that she is holding it together, especially on camera,' I said.

'She is an incredibly strong lady,' Johnny replied. 'We do need to know a bit more about the cocaine side of it, though. That's the reason we are here.'

Minutes later, I was sitting back on the sofa, next to Chanel ready for more questions and answers.

Chanel was great at asking a question in a way which didn't sound too politically correct but still opened people up.

'I know you mentioned earlier, that your son wasn't driving. Did he know his friend was drunk?'

No question seemed too much for her.

'Usually, they would have one or two pints and drive home, so no he didn't. That wasn't the issue. It was the amount of cocaine he had taken.'

'Can you explain a little more?' I asked.

'After the inquest and police reports, it was found that his friend was high on cocaine. When I say high, I mean really high. They said he must have had huge quantities prior to the crash. No drug is worth a life.'

What shocked me the most was what she said after; 'My son's friend did manage to escape the car with only minor injuries.'

The driver who had been responsible for his friend's death had survived, despite being the reason they'd hit that roundabout at a fatal speed. It wasn't a question for the lady in front of us, sitting politely on her sofa, revealing the scar that laid across her life for all to see the moment they looked in her eyes. But I wondered what he felt about it all now. He had to live with the knowledge that his taking of cocaine had led to the death of his friend. What a weight to carry around with you.

We thanked the lady for sharing her experience with us, and despite our kind words and her acceptance of our condolences, it was clear that nothing we said would ever take the pain away from her life. No parent could get over losing a child, and it was made even worse by the wasteful circumstances in which she'd been robbed of her son. We remained professional, detached from her in some way, but it broke me up to hear her story.

When we left, it was late and we were all tired from the interview, both physically and emotionally. Sleep came quickly that night, and a new day had never been more welcome.

Chapter Forty-Six

It was a bright sunny day in Essex, and I was up early and raring to go for another day filming. After such a tough few days, both mentally and physically, I couldn't wait for the final days ahead.

Before I could think about crossing the finishing line, Chanel and I had another interview to conduct. Kent was our location. We'd be meeting a smuggler, only this time he was the guy bringing the drugs into the country, unlike Colombia, where it had been exported from.

With Johnny working pretty much non-stop for two months, it was time for him to have a well-deserved day off. His only job for the day was to drop Chanel and I off at the local train station.

After arriving in Kent almost one hour later, we were greeted at the station by George.

'Hi guys, how was Essex?'

'A little deep really,' I relayed. 'Good interview, but a sad story.'

'Yeah I heard. On a lighter note, we are going to be meeting up with a smuggler tonight.'

'What type of smuggler?' Chanel asked. 'Aeroplane, train or car?'

'Actually Chanel, it's a guy who imports it, mostly on huge ships.'

'This is my forte,' I said. 'Interviewing boat drivers.'

'No Louis, this will be something completely different.' George said. 'We will be meeting him very close to the sea, but not on a boat.'

Later that evening, we'd arrived at a pier somewhere in Kent. I'd never been to Kent prior to the trip so I had no idea where I was. I'd always imagined Kent to be the place for spectacular beaches. I didn't know it was an area used to import cocaine, but who would?

With George, Chanel, the sound engineer and myself sat in the car patiently waiting, George went over the plan for the interview.

'When our guy arrives, we'll make our way over to him. Marc has met up with him prior, so we shouldn't have too much to worry about. He knows what questions we may ask, so I'm guessing he will be prepared.'

When I was eighteen years old, I remember sitting in my car with friends in a car park, just off Blackpool pier. Two men knocked on the door and began shouting. I quickly started my engine and drove off. I didn't have fond memories of waiting in car parks near a pier, so I was a little worried the same may happen again.

'He will be wearing a balaclava,' George continued, 'But don't let that put you off. It's for his own protection. Is there anything you would like to ask me?'

I had many questions, but at this late stage in the trip I didn't bother. I just wanted the scene to go smoothly and to get back to the car safely.

As if by coincidence, a man knocked on the car window. I almost shit my pants. He didn't say a word and started walking towards the pier in pitch black. The night was extremely cold, and as each step he took, I could see his breath fading away.

George was as ready as us.

'I think that's him. Let's make a move.'

It was almost 1 a.m. and the day had consisted of waiting around for this one very guy. I was hoping it was him and not some random person knocking on car windows. As we made our way down the unlit pier, I started imagining the worst. What if he has a gun, kills us all and throws us over the edge of the pier. But why would he do that?

Many thoughts like that flashed through my head throughout the journey. I think it was to do with the nature of the programme and the criminals we met.

After walking down the pier at an almost snail speed, we'd reached our man. George and the sound engineer began to chat with him, whilst me and Chanel rested on the edge looking awkwardly out to sea. Then suddenly, the balaclava was placed over his head and the cameras were rolling. The interview had started, and I instantly questioned his position in the drugs trade.

'You see the huge ships behind you? I use them to bring in large quantities of cocaine?' He replied.

I was a little confused. 'What? The ones docked behind us?'

He said whilst laughing. 'Not that exact one, but a ship very similar.'

We'd only been interviewing him for a matter of seconds and I almost felt a sense of relief that he had a funny humour.

'I have contacts in Spain and all over Europe. I can have it delivered to anywhere in the UK by ship. Obviously not for you 'Mancs', but most places.'

Chanel shouted whilst giggling. 'I'm from Bristol actually.'

George stopped the cameras. I think he was a little worried that the interview was coming across a little too friendly. We weren't there to make friends, we were there to do a job.

As we continued, Chanel asked him; 'So, once the cocaine arrives at the port, how does it then end up in your hands?'

'I have divers, they will go underneath the both, collect the cocaine and deliver it to me. Well not to me personally, I wouldn't be that daft to touch it, but you get what I mean.'

I, like Chanel was stunned; 'Wait, divers?'

'Yeah, the cocaine is stored underneath the ship and waterproofed, that way it's very hard to detect.' I was baffled.

After informing us that the goods were shipped from Spain to Kent, where it would arrive in kilogram packages, each drop being worth around one-hundred-thousand pounds. I had no idea how the producers had made contact with him. With eight drops a year, he was earning big money.

He was no small fish. He was a shark in the sea of the cocaine trade, and he told us that he wasn't afraid to kill someone if they stepped out of line and jeopardised a deal. He was in charge of a lot of people, mainly men, and after telling us divers were sent into the water to retrieve the cocaine after the drop, he, like the Colombian smuggler seemed to have very similar tactics. I'd known that the cocaine trade was huge above sea level, but I had never suspected the battle continued underwater.

It was time to leave, we were shattered, and the guy left us looking as fresh as a daisy. For us it was the end of an adventure, but for him, it was just another day.

Chapter Forty-Seven

After two months of filming, I woke up for the final day and it felt strange. I knew there was little chance of me ever having an experience like it again. The adventure already felt like it was over and as I struggled to get out of bed, I received a WhatsApp message from Marc.

'Hi all. As you know this is it, the final day of filming. The plan for today is to head to the studio for the final interviews. We will then have some lunch and say our goodbyes.'

Receiving the message just reminded me how sad I was for the journey to end. Meeting the crew, the cast and even the criminals was something I would never forget and hopefully something I could one day tell my kids and grandkids, not that I used cocaine in the past, but about the people I'd met and how it affected my future choices.

Shortly after meeting up with Chanel, Troi and Amber downstairs, I could see the sadness in everyone's faces. As we sat down for breakfast, table-talk was minimal. Marc arrived minutes later.

'Is everyone ready to go?'

Chanel replied whilst laughing.

'Not really, can we not carry on a little longer?' Which made Marc giggle.

'Just wait till you watch it back, it's something what will live in your memories forever.'

It was time to check-out of the hotel and head into central London for the final day. An hour later, we reached the filming studio to be welcomed at the entrance by Johnny, George and a few other members of the production company. It was the final time we'd be all together as one big crew.

Still totally unaware of how the final interviews were going to work, the crew invited the four of us to take a seat in the green room.

Chanel looked over to me sat opposite her.

'This looks a bit serious.'

Johnny spoke first.

'Firstly, I want to thank you for the past two months working with us. Marc, George and I can't wait to get in the editing suite to put the final touches to the show. I think you will be really surprised by how it looks. There are a few final things we need to do today which is the reason you are here.'

Suddenly there was a little tension in the room. At this point I thought we'd been pranked. 'Before you started this journey,' Johnny continued, 'you had all admitted to taking cocaine in the past. We'd now like to know if any of your opinions have changed after everything you have seen? Before you answer, keep your thoughts to yourself for the final interviews.'

George stepped in.

'Yes, I just want to re-iterate what Johnny has said. It's been a real pleasure working with the four of you. I'm sure we've made a great show and it's been one of the best projects I've worked on.'

Next up was Marc.

'Although I wasn't with you guys whilst in Colombia, I have looked back at most of the things you have done, and it looks fantastic. Even the sections in the UK look spectacular. I can't wait to see the final edit.'

We all felt a sense of relief that filming was almost over, so much so that we popped open a bottle of champagne. What was left to do was still unknown, but at this point nothing phased me. Well I thought it didn't until I was invited into the studio to film my closing part. Again, like my initial interview back in London on the first day, they had a chair set up waiting on my arrival with huge bright lights focused only on me. The pressure was on.

With Johnny, George and Marc sat directly behind the camera, all I could see was the shadow of their faces on the dark walls around me.

'Ok, so like the very first initial interview, I'd like you to answer in full answers please,' said Johnny.

Lights, camera and action, one last time.

'Can you tell me what part of the journey you have enjoyed the most Louis?'

I replied with a sign of sadness – 'The best part of my journey had to be meeting up with the children at the Favelas. Something has just stuck with me since leaving there. Although there wasn't too much focus on the cocaine side, I felt I learnt a lot.'

It was so hard to stay focused knowing that it was the very last interview. Johnny continued to fire questions at me. Most of them I'd answered throughout filming, but the one which stuck out the most was the penultimate question - 'Do you think talking about cocaine with your family has brought you closer?'

The question made me swallow heavily. I could have never imagined prior to filming the show that I would ever discuss cocaine with my parents, let alone filming a TV documentary on it.

I realised that it had.

'I suppose in a way the show has brought us closer. I wouldn't say it has anything to do with them knowing I'd taken cocaine in the past; it's probably just made the conversation a lot easier to discuss. I would recommend though, anyone who is slightly nervous about talking about cocaine with their parents, don't be, it's not all that bad.'

My final question was the one I'd be considering for the whole two months I'd been filming. I knew I'd get asked it eventually. George was the one to go ahead – 'Ok final question Louis. If you were to be offered cocaine now, after everything you have seen, would you take it?'

I knew this would be one of the main questions which would be edited and shown to the public. I had to be one-hundred percent honest.

'After everything I have seen, from Colombia to the UK I'd like to say I'd never do it again, but...'

The shadows were still. The lights were hot. Sometimes you're aware of the weight of certain questions... and answers. I knew that my family would be watching. But I had to be truthful. 'I think never is a strong word.'

Those were my final words. After leaving the studio, I regretted my final answer, simply because I knew it wouldn't be the answer my family would be looking for. But I'd been true to my word. I was never going to categorically say 'never', as I knew if there was a time that I decided to dabble in it again, on a night out or at a festival, then I'd have lied to myself... and them. Just like I'd discovered in Colombia, from the jungle to the mean streets and Favelas and shadows in between, it was all a question of perspective. If you looked at cocaine as a party drug, what harm did it do other than to the person taking it, a responsible adult making a decision, just for themselves? However, if you viewed cocaine as a gateway to an industry of drug-trafficking, export and danger that impacted on everyone from children in villages to families, then it wasn't something worth contemplating for a second.

I'd learned about the addictive nature of cocaine, the impact to a person's health, from their nose to their heart. But it was like anything in the end - a personal choice.

Where do you draw the line?